CITYPACK
Beijing

By Sean Sheehan

Fodor's

Fodor's Travel Publications, Inc.
New York • Toronto • London • Sydney • Auckland

WWW.FODORS.COM

Contents

About this book

KEY TO SYMBOLS

✚	map reference on the fold-out map accompanying this book (see below)	🚌	nearest bus route
✉	address	🚢	nearest riverboat or ferry stop
☎	telephone number	♿	facilities for visitors with disabilities
🕓	opening times	✋	admission charge
🍴	restaurant or café on premises or nearby	↔	other nearby places of interest
Ⓜ	nearest subway station	❓	tours, lectures, or special events
🚆	nearest train station	➤	cross-reference (see below)
		ℹ	tourist information

ORGANIZATION

Citypack Beijing's six sections cover the six most important aspects of your visit to Beijing. This book includes:

- Beijing life—the city and its people
- Itineraries, a walk, a bicycle ride and excursions—how to organize your time
- The top 25 sights—plotted from west to east
- Features about different aspects of the city that make it special
- Detailed listings of restaurants, hotels, shops and nightlife
- Practical information

In addition, text boxes provide fascinating extra facts and snippets, highlights of places to visit and invaluable practical advice.

CROSS-REFERENCES

To help you make the most of your visit, cross-references, indicated by ➤, show you where to find additional information about a place or subject.

MAPS

- **The fold-out map** in the wallet at the back of the book is a comprehensive street plan of Beijing. All the map references given in the book refer to this map. For example, the Hall of Supreme Harmony in the Forbidden City has the following information: ✚ **G6** – indicating the grid square of the map in which the Hall of Supreme Harmony will be found.
- **The city-center maps** on the inside front and back covers of the book itself are for quick reference. They show the Top 25 Sights, described on pages 24–48, which are clearly plotted by number (**1** – **25**, not page number) from west to east.

PRICES

Where appropriate, an indication of the cost of an establishment is given by **$** signs: **$$$** denotes higher prices, **$$** denotes average prices, while **$** denotes lower charges.

BEIJING
life

INTRODUCING BEIJING

A word of advice

Beijing is changing fast in many ways. Be aware that hotels, restaurants, clubs and bars can close, move or change name more rapidly than in most cities. In addition, few people speak English, except in tourist hotels. If you wish to visit any establishment in this guide, ask a member of staff at your hotel to telephone and check that it is still open and at the same address. The same person can then make a reservation on your behalf if necessary.

All cities develop and change, but what is happening in Beijing is astonishing.. All the troublesome aspects of a visit in the 1980s have faded into the background. You no longer need special certificates to go shopping; the difficulty of even finding a store to make a simple purchase of fresh fruit or aspirin is now a quaint memory. Buses are impossibly overcrowded still, but inexpensive taxis are commonplace and finding your way around is more straightforward. In the old days, even finding a decent place to eat could be a challenge.

Beijing, chosen in 1260 by Kublai Khan as his winter residence and now capital to a nation of over one billion people, is undergoing profound changes. When you spend time in the city you have the unique opportunity to observe a social revolution every bit as radical as Mao Zedong's 1960s Cultural Revolution. You still encounter old Beijing even on main thoroughfares: A bicycle repairer squats on a street corner with his tools, waiting for a passing bicyclist with a puncture; down an adjoining *hutong* (alley or lane) people still insulate the walls of their homes with newspaper. But evidence of a new society is everywhere. Beijingers are embracing consumerism with revolutionary fervor. Signs and menus appear in English, cellular phones are commonplace, Western-style shopping malls and office

Consumerism has arrived in Beijing

complexes are being developed at an amazing rate. The people of Beijing are sampling what the West has to offer and observing the process is enthralling.

Despite these changes, it is China's 3,000-year-old civilization that remains at the heart of Beijing's appeal. During over 800 years, the city has been home to 33 emperors of four great dynasties, whose rich legacy includes such major sites as the Forbidden City and the Great Wall. More recent triumphs and tragedies are enshrined in Tian'anmen Square, one of the more controversial stops on 1998's Presidential visit to Beijing. You can also experience China's ancient culture in more living forms: Restaurants specializing in regional cuisines open a window on one of the world's most incredible food cultures; traditional teahouses are reopening; Chinese opera is back in favor, and every evening a theater plays host to the 2,000-year-old tradition of acrobatics. What prompted the early waves of independent travelers in the 1980s was the expectation of seeing all of this and experiencing at first hand a culture that had shunned the West. This is still the chief draw, but now it can be enjoyed with the benefit of creature comforts, and is made even more astonishing by the city's social renaissance. Beijing has flung its doors wide open. Go in.

Where is China going?

Economic reform is transforming China at an astonishing rate—but at a price. State-run industries that lose money are being closed down, resulting in massive unemployment and social unrest. Uncertainty is growing over the ability of the banking system to handle the country's financial and economic revolution. Political dissent has been crushed for the time being, but can the political order remain immune to change? No one really knows.

The older generation has witnessed another revolution

A DAY IN THE LIFE OF A BEIJINGER

"Early to bed and early to rise" is as true of Beijing today as in imperial times, when giant bells rang out the hour of dawn from the towers of the Forbidden City. In the days of Mao Zedong, every home had an alarm clock painted with a revolutionary theme (they can still be picked up for a few pounds from enterprising vendors) and people woke up ideologically fit for a hard day's labor. Beijingers nowadays still rise with the sun and if you do too, you should visit the public park nearest your hotel one morning, before 8AM, to see Beijingers of all ages performing tai chi. This Chinese form of calisthenics is spiritual in nature (▶ 52), as opposed to the modern dancing sessions that also take place early in the morning as a form of physical exercise. One consequence of most Beijingers making an early start is that lunch happens around noon and evening meals are over by

Early morning dance in Tiantan Park

6:30. Afterwards, time must be allowed for housework, for there are no stay-at-home housewives. (Do not be fooled by the presence of familiar advertisements for labor-saving household appliances—most homes do not have washing machines, vacuum cleaners or the like.)

Usually, both members of a married couple work outside the home, and they are only likely to have time together on weekends. Sunday is a day off work for most employees and, in a city of over 11 million people, that means heavy-duty shopping (for this reason, try sightseeing rather than shopping in Beijing on Sundays if you can).

It is more common for one adult in the family to leave state employment and work for a private enterprise, perhaps in a hotel, while the other stays within the state system for security. But for how long? They have heard the stories of massive unemployment in state industries outside the capital, and feel they are lucky to have a job.

Family survey

The average income for an urban family in China is 14,000 yuan, according to a 1997 survey. For Beijingers the figure is likely to be a little higher because of the greater opportunities to work in the private market. The survey also revealed that residents of the capital have the most cash under their mattresses—around 24,000 yuan per family.

BEIJING IN FIGURES

THE PLACE

- Beijing's total area is nearly 6,562 sq. miles, roughly that of Belgium. The city limits (including rural areas) extend for 31 miles
- The city is one of the few world capitals not situated on a coast or navigable river
- Beijing is roughly on the same latitude as Rome, Madrid and Philadelphia

THE PEOPLE

- Beijing is home to 1 in 100 Chinese people
- The official population exceeds 11 million
- All of China's 56 nationalities are represented in Beijing, but the Han people account for over 96 percent of the city's population
- The Chinese language is a series of dialects, mutually incomprehensible to the ear even though they share a common set of characters. To facilitate communication between Chinese from different regions, the dialect of Beijing has emerged as the basis for a common spoken language. Known as Mandarin, *putonghua* to the Chinese, it is learned by non-Beijingers as a second language

Chinese characters are difficult to master but street signs are romanized

SURPRISES

- A 1995 municipal law decrees that no dog taller than 14 inches can be legally raised in Beijing
- During the 1995 UN Women's Conference, a temporary law, now rescinded, was enacted forbidding residents to hang laundry from windows
- "So great a number of houses and of people, no man could tell the number..." What Marco Polo observed in the 13th century still seems true today
- Beijing's railroad station can hold up to 14,000 people on its platforms – more than any other railroad station in the world
- Some 9 million bikes are pressed into service each morning across the city. In a sign of changing times, bicycle thefts have jumped by 700 percent in recent years, and in 1996 some 80,000 were stolen

A CHRONOLOGY

700BC Mongols, Koreans and local Chinese conduct trade where the capital is now located, and its position on the southern edge of the North China Plain attracts military leaders.

AD1215 Mongol warrior Genghis Khan captures a small town called Youzhou (Tranquil City) and his grandson Kublai establishes his capital in the renamed Dadu (Great Capital) by the end of the century. Marco Polo is astonished at the wealth derived from its position at the start of the Silk Road.

1368 The Mongols are defeated and the Ming dynasty established. The capital moves south to Nanjing, but the second Ming emperor returns and, building the Forbidden City and the Temple of Heaven (Tiantan), becomes the great architect of Beijing.

1644 The Manchus establish the Qing dynasty and develop and expand the capital over the next century. The great Summer Palace is laid out and built north of the city.

1860 Anglo-French troops attack Beijing and burn the Summer Palace during the Opium Wars. In 1884, Dowager Cixi misappropriates funds earmarked for the navy and orders the building of a new Summer Palace. Hermetically sealed within the Forbidden City, she is cut off from the real world and oblivious to the poverty and discontent that is spreading through the country.

1911 Successive waves of occupation by foreign troops weaken the imperial order and the Manchus are overthrown. The Nationalist Party takes power and the Republic of China is established with Sun Yat Sen as president.

1928 Beijing is under the control of Chiang Kai Shek before falling to the Japanese in 1937. After 1945, following the defeat of the Japanese, the civil war that began in 1927 resumes between Chiang and Mao Zedong's Communists.

1949 | In Beijing the victorious Mao announces the People's Republic of China and the remnants of Chiang's Nationalists flee to Taiwan. Soviet experts help the Chinese tear down and rebuild large parts of Beijing.

1966 | Beijing is the scene for the start of the Cultural Revolution, Mao's master move in a power struggle within the Communist Party. Red Guards wave their little red books and the country's schools and universities remain closed for a decade.

1976 | Mao dies and, soon after, Deng Xiaoping takes power. Westerners are admitted into the country, and special economic zones are created, allowing foreign investment.

1989 | Students mass in Tian'anmen Square to demand political liberalization. The government cracks down on dissent by calling in the army. Hundreds—possibly thousands—are shot down.

1997 | Deng's death leaves Jiang Zemin as paramount leader, and he witnesses the return of Hong Kong to Chinese rule.

1998 | Life in Beijing seems stable, but there are major economic and political problems as the country deals with the transition to capitalism while retaining one-party rule.

Traditional Chinese music remains popular in this fast-changing culture

11

PEOPLE & EVENTS FROM HISTORY

Mao's Little Red Book *was read zealously in the 1960s*

China's architect

When Emperor Yongle, the 26th son of the first Ming emperor took the reins of the dynasty in 1403, he moved the capital north from Nanjing to the older city of Dadu, strategically closer to the Mongols. At the beginning of the Ming era, Dadu had become Beiping ("northern peace"), but Yongle rechristened it Beijing ("northern capital") and called in geomancers to advise on the building of a new imperial palace (the Forbidden City) and a sacrificial temple (Tiantan). The layout of Beijing has remained largely unchanged since the days of Yongle.

EMPRESS DOWAGER CIXI (1834–1908)

Cixi first entered the Forbidden City as a concubine to a Manchu emperor. When he died in 1861, she became regent to their infant son. From then until her death, she was the effective ruler of China—a deeply conservative figure who was renowned, among other things, for releasing 10,000 caged birds each year on her birthday. She acquired the nickname "Old Buddha," and following her son's death chose her nephew to be emperor. When he tried to introduce reforms, she had him confined to the palace as a virtual prisoner. The day before she herself died, she organized his murder.

MAO ZEDONG (1893–1976)

The son of a well-to-do farmer in the Hunan province, Mao adapted Marxism to suit rural China. When his fellow communists were threatened by Chiang Kai Shek, he organized the famous year-long, 5,890 mile Long March across 18 mountain ranges and 24 rivers to escape capture. After he proclaimed the People's Republic in 1949, his policies dominated Chinese life until 1976. Despite official acknowledgement that Mao made some mistakes, he remains a deeply revered figure among the older Chinese and his influence continues to be felt.

TIAN'ANMEN SQUARE PROTEST
(June 4, 1989)

When students at Beijing University began occupying Tian'anmen Square to protest at the growing corruption and lack of political reform, they gained support from the people of Beijing. When the authorities turned a deaf ear to their complaints, some 3,000 students went on a hunger strike. By early June, 1989, the government had brought in troops who could be trusted to obey orders and resist pleas from citizens who begged them not to attack their own people. In the early hours of June 4, the troops moved into the square, shooting and running over protesters with their tanks. Hospitals were ordered not to treat casualties. No official casualty count has ever been released.

BEIJING
how to organize your time

ITINERARIES

In Beijing, planning your time is essential, especially if it's limited. You really need at least three days, but a longer stay, which allows time not only for seeing some of the major sites but also for slowing down and observing some aspects of Beijing life, is much more worthwhile.

ITINERARY ONE	**THE FORBIDDEN CITY & THE SILK MARKET**
Morning	Start early with a visit to the Forbidden City (➤ 31), entering through Meridian Gate (➤ 51) and leaving by way of Shenwu Gate (➤ 51). If time and energy allow, cross the street outside to visit Jingshan Park (➤ 30).
Afternoon	Go shopping in the Silk Market (➤ 75) and the Friendship Store (➤ 74), a short walk away to the west. Take a taxi or walk further west to Tian'anmen Square (➤ 38) for the flag lowering ceremony at dusk.
Evening	Catch the exhilarating China Acrobatic Troupe at the Chaoyang Theater (➤ 82) or stroll along Wangfujing and take in the Forbidden City at night (➤ 18).
ITINERARY TWO	**TIANTAN PARK & SANLITUN**
Morning	Start early enough that you can reach Tiantan Park in time to see Beijingers practicing tai chi (➤ 8) before visiting the Qinian Hall (Hall of Prayer for Good Harvests ➤ 44) and the Imperial Vault of Heaven (➤ 45) within the park. Leave by the east gate, passing the Tiantan Market stalls which sell cultural curios from the 1960s (➤ 77). Then, if time allows, cross the street to the Hongqiao Market (➤ 73), where pearls, arts and crafts items, and antiques are for sale.
Afternoon	Visit the Sanlitun area (➤ 75) for shopping and fit in a reconnaissance of the restaurants (➤ 64–9), bars and clubs (➤ 78–81) you may want to visit in the evening.
Evening	Return to Sanlitun.

ITINERARY THREE	**THE GREAT WALL**
Morning & Afternoon	Join a day-long tour (booked ahead if possible) to the Great Wall (► 27) and Ming Tombs (► 28). Tours usually include lunch.
Evening	Visit the Beijing Concert Hall for classical Chinese music or take in one of the dinner shows with a Beijing roast duck meal (► 82–3).
ITINERARY FOUR	**THE SUMMER PALACE**
Morning	Visit the Summer Palace (► 24), or spend the morning in Tian'anmen Square (► 38) visiting the Chairman Mao Memorial Hall (► 41) and the Museum of the Chinese Revolution (► 43). For something more active, join the masses on two wheels and rent a bicycle for a tour north of the city center (► 17).
Afternoon	Experience the Beijing underground by heading for the Yonghegong (Lama Temple, ► 47) or visit the quieter Great Bell Temple (► 26).
Evening	Enjoy an evening of cultural entertainment at the Lao She Teahouse (► 83) or return to Tian'anmen Square for a stroll through the lonely expanse of Beijing's political heart.

9 million bikes are used daily in Beijing

WALK

INFORMATION

Distance 1 mile
Time About 2 hours including sights
Start point Opposite Bank of China on Fuchengmennei Dajie
➕ D5
🚇 Fuchengmen
End point Bank of China on Fuchengmennei Dajie
➕ D5

OFF THE TOURIST TRAIL

This walk shows workaday life for ordinary Beijingers as they go about their daily business. It also provides an opportunity to visit several lesser-known places of cultural interest that might otherwise be overlooked.

From Fuchengmen subway station, walk the short distance to the junction with Fuchengmennei Dajie, cross the street and turn right for the first stop at the Lu Xun museum. (Look for an English sign in blue, pointing the way to a municipal government department, just before a Kentucky Fried Chicken restaurant.) A cobbler and food vendors have stalls down this side street on the left; the museum is at the end. Continue along Fuchengmennei Dajie and look for a store at No. 165 selling medicines. The Nepalese-style White Pagoda Temple, which towers over this section of the street, is reached by turning down the *hutong* (alley) at No. 165.

Back on the main street, you pass a high school (which used to be a temple) opposite a large red wall on the other side of the street. Head straight ahead across the junction. At No. 25 there is the entrance to the Guangjisi Temple. At this point, either retrace your steps, or hop on a No. 101, 103 or 42 bus, which will take you back to the

Guangjishi Temple dates from the 12th century

starting point, where there are refreshment possibilities. There is an Indian restaurant (► 67) in Holiday Inn Downtown, which also offers an inexpensive lunch buffet of international cuisine, and a Kenny Rogers restaurant next door. The Vantone New World Shopping Center (► 76) has a burger restaurant.

BICYCLE RIDE

PARKS & LAKES

A bicycle tour gives the satisfying feeling of experiencing an essential aspect of Beijing life. You can rent a bicycle at most hotels .

Head south down Wangfujing Dajie and turn left on to Dongchang'an Jie and left again on to Dongdanbei Dajie. Bike north up this name-changing road for 2½ miles, almost to the Yonghegong (Lama Temple), near the main junction with the Second Ring Road, Andingmendong Dajie (⊞ J2). Turn left into Guozijian Jie, a small street which heads west past the Temple of Confucius. Bike down this street to the T-junction with Andingmennei Dajie. Turn left, and at the traffic lights turn right on to Guloudong Dajie (⊞ H3), continuing to a junction by a large red building, Drum Tower. Turn left here on to Di'Anmenwai Dajie. A few hundred yards after a McDonald's restaurant, turn right on to a lane, immediately after a humped bridge.

Fine detail from the Lama Temple

Follow the lane down to the lake and keep the water on your right as far as Di'Anmenxi Dajie (⊞ G4). The rear entrance to Beihai Park is across the street. Turn left on to Di'Anmenxi Dajie and at the first junction with traffic lights, turn right to rejoin Di'Anmenwai Dajie (the street with the humped bridge). Bike south to the T-junction at the edge of Jingshan Park, turn left on to Jingshanhou Jie and follow the street around the park (there is an entrance on your right) to another T-junction (⊞ G5). Go left on to Jingshanqian Jie and after passing the China Art Gallery turn right back on to Wangfujing. A picnic lunch from a supermarket, could be enjoyed in one of the parks. Note: To stay safe, always use the bicycle lanes.

THE SIGHTS

- ● Yonghegong (Lama Temple, ▶ 47)
- ● Temple of Confucius (▶ 46)
- ● Beihai Park (▶ 29)
- ● Jingshan Park (▶ 30)
- ● Forbidden City (▶ 31)
- ● China Art Gallery (▶ 54)

INFORMATION

Distance 6 miles
Time About 3 hours
Start/end point Wangfujing Dajie
⊞ H5
▣ 104, 211

EVENING STROLLS

Street stalls selling western-style takeaway snacks are still uncommon

INFORMATION

Wangfujing
Distance 1.8 miles
Time About 1 hour excluding refreshment
Start point Beijing Hotel
➕ H7
🚍 1, 4, 10, 37, 42, 57, 203
End point North of Forbidden City
➕ G5
🚍 101, 103, 109, 111

Ritan Park
Distance 1 mile
Time 1 hour
Start/end point Jianguomen subway station
➕ K6
Ⓜ Jianguomen

WANGFUJING

From the Beijing Hotel, turn left on to Wangfujing Dajie. The Beijing Department Store (► 76) and the Foreign Languages Bookstore (► 77) are both worth a browse. Try to reach the main junction with traffic lights around 6PM, when eating takes on a new dimension and you'll get a healthy dose of culture shock at the open-air food stalls down Dong'anmen Dajie. Further up Wangfujing, on the other side of the street, the Crowne Prince Hotel has a small art gallery off the foyer and further up, at No. 26, the delightful Banpo Beer Hut (► 62) offers refreshment. At the top of Wangfujing turn left and walk as far as the moat for a night view of the Forbidden City.

RITAN PARK

From Jianguomen subway station, head east along Jianguomenwai Dajie and turn left at the International Club. The Russian Market (► 74) may still be open, but the entrance to Ritan Park (► 52) is on the other side of the street. Go straight through the park as far as the circular walled area and then go right, keeping the playground on the left, before exiting on to Guanghua Lu and turning left. When you reach the British embassy, cross over and turn right onto Xiushuidong Jie for a rear approach to the Silk Market (► 75). Alternatively, proceed as far as the traffic lights and turn right onto Dongdaqiao Lu for drinks and food (► 68). Either journey will lead back on to Jianguomenwai Dajie for a stroll back to the station.

ORGANIZED SIGHTSEEING

If your time is limited, you may want to consider an organized tour, especially to sites outside the city like the Great Wall and the Ming Tombs (▶ 27, 28). Most hotels have a tour desk where you can make reservations. Prices vary, so shop around.

EAS TRAVEL

This organization, also known as the China Civil International Tourist Corporation, offers various tours and assistance with most other aspects of a visit to the city, including accommodations.

✉ Bridge Mansion, 28 Dongsanhuanbei Lu, Chaoyang District ☎ 6594 6161; fax 6592 6717; e-mail eastvl@nihao.com. Web site at www.nihao.com/eastravel

CITS

China International Travel Service desks can be found at the Jing Guang New World, Great Wall Sheraton, Kempinski and Hilton hotels. CITS conducts a variety of tours, including a busy day tour by bus (Mon, Wed, Fri, and Sat, 8:30AM) that visits the major sights: Tian'anmen Square, the Forbidden City, the Summer Palace and the Imperial Vault of Heaven. Also available is a 7AM "Morning Exercises with Local Chinese" tour. CITS tours tend to be more impersonal than those from EAS Travel.

✉ 28 Jianguomenwai Dajie, Chaoyang District ☎ 6515 8565; fax 6515 7798

In imperial times huge pots in the Forbidden City were filled with water in case of fire

Sample prices

A typical CITS city tour by bus like the one mentioned at left is currently around 340 yuan per person, including lunch, admission and tour guide. A morning-only city tour usually costs around 120 yuan and a trip to the Great Wall is 200 yuan. The *hutong* tour mentioned bottom left costs around 180 yuan per person.

BEIJING HUTONG TOURIST AGENCY

Tours of the *hutongs* (ancient city alleys or lanes) start at 8:50AM and 1:50PM from the agency's office at the rear entrance of Beihai Park.

✉ 26 Di'anmenxi Dajie, Xicheng District ☎ 6615 9097/6400 2787

EXCURSIONS

Little bells tinkle to murmurs in the wind

INFORMATION

**Fragrant Hills Park
(Xiangshan Gongyuan)**
Distance 12½ miles west of Beijing
Journey time About 50 minutes
- 🚌 333 from the Summer
  Palace; 360 from the zoo
  (► 60); 318 from
  Pingguoyuan
- ☎ 6259 1155
- 🕙 6AM–7PM
- 🎟 Inexpensive

Marco Polo Bridge (Lugouqiao)
Distance 10 miles south of Beijing
Journey time About 45 minutes
  by bus
- 🚌 339
- ✉ Wanping City, Fengtai District
- ☎ 6381 5981
- 🕙 6AM–9PM
- 🎟 Inexpensive

FRAGRANT HILLS PARK

Popular with Beijingers as well as tourists, this accessible destination offers fresh air, bracing walks and superb views of the countryside from the top of the highest peak, reached by chairlift or on foot. Once royal hunting territory, this was where Mao Zedong and his revolutionaries lived before moving to Beijing in 1949. Highlights include botanical gardens and the Temple of Brilliance (Zhao Miao), which, uniquely, escaped destruction by foreign troops in 1860 and 1900. Near the north gate entrance, the Indian-style Azure Clouds Temple (Biyun Si) is well worth visiting if only for the visual brilliance of its stupas (Buddhist tiered towers). Inside, there is a display relating to Sun Yat Sen (► 10), whose body was kept here for a while before being moved in the 1920s.

MARCO POLO BRIDGE

The fact that Marco Polo never mentioned the Great Wall is one reason scholars question whether he ever made it to China. The Western name of this bridge derives from his putative 1290 visit and his detailed description of the bridge. Spanning the River Yongding, it was built in 1192 and restored in the 17th century, and is noted for an 18th-century stele with a calligraphic inscription by Emperor Qianlong. On each side of the bridge is a parapet with hundreds of carved lions surmounting the columns. In 1937 the bridge witnessed the opening shots in the war against the Japanese invasion. A museum nearby is devoted to this event.

TIANJIN

There are two main attractions in China's fourth largest city and Beijing's nearest port: a wealth of colonial architecture, and superb antiques shopping. The old part of town, south of the main railroad station, has a number of old

Careful restoration has recreated these Fragrant Hills Park structures

INFORMATION

Tianjin

Distance 50 miles east of Beijing

Journey time 2 hours by bus or express train from Beijing

🚌 Buses depart from outside Beijing railroad station

✉ There is no tourist office in Tianjin but the CITS office, 22 Yonyi Lu (opposite the Friendship Store), may be of some help.

☎ 022-8358 349/8358 501

❓ Organized trips from Beijing are available through CITS (► 19)

Peking Man

Distance 37 miles southwest of Beijing

Journey time About 2 hours by bus

🚌 From Haihutun bus station (get off in the village of Zhoukoudian), or by train from Yongdingmen railroad station in Beijing

✉ Zhoukoudian, Fangshan District

☎ 6930 1272

🕐 8:30–4:30

💵 Inexpensive

buildings dating back to the 19th century, when European imperial powers established themselves in the wake of a "treaty" imposed by the British. The antiques market, based around Shenyang Jie, is especially worth a visit on weekends when the streets are flooded with merchandise ranging from genuine antiques to inexpensive Mao memorabilia and related knick-knacks. Try to arrive on Saturday so as to catch the Sunday morning market around 9AM.

PEKING MAN SITE & MUSEUM

In 1921, excavations near the village of Zhoukoudian revealed evidence of palaeolithic Man—*Homo erectus Pekinensis*—dating back over 500,000 years. Bones of more than 40 individuals were identified. You can wander around the original site and, in an adjoining museum, see replicas of anthropological finds and remains of extinct creatures that must have terrified Peking Man. The original skull of Peking Man disappeared during World War II, when it was taken out of the country for safekeeping.

WHAT'S ON

JANUARY

Spring Festival Concert: In the Beijing Concert Hall (➤ 82). Classical Chinese music.

FEBRUARY

Chinese New Year: The most important festival in the Chinese calendar, falling in late January or early February, on the first day of the first moon. Celebrations are held in the Great Bell Temple (➤ 26), Ditan Park (➤ 52) and elsewhere. It is very much a family affair.

Lantern Festival: Also governed by the lunar cycle, it usually falls in February or March. One of the most colorful festivals; families celebrate in the evenings, especially in parks, with lanterns, which are carried by hand and placed on the ground around picnicking groups.

MARCH/APRIL

Guanyin's Birthday: A good time to visit temples. (Guanyin is the goddess of mercy.)

APRIL

Martial Arts Festival: Special martial displays make this a good time to visit the Great Wall at Badaling (➤ 27).

Tomb Sweeping Day/Clear Brightness Festival (April 5 most years, April 4 in leap years): Relatives pay their respects to their ancestors by sweeping and cleaning their tombs and burning "ghost money."

MAY

May Day (May 1): International Labor Day is marked by splendid floral displays citywide and celebrations in Tian'anmen Square.

Youth Day: (May 4): Also marked by floral displays.

SEPTEMBER

China Arts Festival: Organized by the Ministry of Culture (☎ 6403 1059). Details in the *China Daily*.

Mid-Fall Festival: Marked by the giving of moon cakes, filled with a mixture of sweets and savories—an acquired taste.

OCTOBER

National Day (October 1): The founding of the People's Republic of China is marked by colorful flags, bunting, and red lanterns. Every five years (October 1999: 50th anniversary of the Liberation) an impressive military display takes place in Tian'anmen Square.

BEIJING's
top 25 sights

The sights are shown on the maps on the inside front cover and inside back cover, numbered **1–25** *from west to east across the city*

23

1

SUMMER PALACE (YIHEYUAN)

A Summer Palace dragon

Here is the largest imperial garden in China, strewn with palaces and architectural flights of fancy. The playgrounds of modern millionaires seem unimaginative in comparison with these pleasure grounds of the royal court.

History Members of Beijing's imperial court needed a summer resort away from the Forbidden City and selected an area northwest of the city for this purpose. What you see today was laid out in the 18th century, but it was toward the end of the following century that Empress Dowager Cixi (➤ 12) misappropriated funds intended for the navy and spent it instead on a lavish rebuilding program for her Summer Palace. Mindful, perhaps, of her debt to the navy, she commissioned the Marble Boat (a wooden paddleboat structure on a marble base) that is berthed at the edge of the lake. The Summer Palace suffered in 1900 at the hands of Anglo-French troops intent on revenge after the Boxer Rebellion, but rebuilding began soon after. A major restoration was completed in the 1950s.

Walking guide After entering the grounds through the East Gate, note first the Hall of Benevolence and Longevity, where Cixi conducted official business with diplomats and courtiers. Stretched out behind the hall is the expanse of Kunming Lake. Keep it on your left, passing the Hall of Jade Ripples before entering the painted Long Corridor. Near the end of this walkway are a coffee shop, the Marble Boat, and a jetty where boat rides and rowboats (or, in winter, skates) are available for trips to the 17-arched bridge, which stretches from the shore to South Lake Island.

OLD SUMMER PALACE

Today's visitors are enchanted by the evocative 865-acre grounds and ruins of the original Summer Palace. Stand quietly and you can imagine fabulously clothed emperors and empresses, attended by scores of servants, at play in the maze.

East meets West Remnants of baroque pillars and the ruins of grand fountains provide a tantalizing hint of the artistic exuberance and sheer splendor that once characterized this royal playground. It was the creation of Emperor Qianlong in the second half of the 18th century and, though ostensibly created as an act of devotion to his mother, his project took on the feel of an audacious architectural binge. The emperor made half a dozen journeys south of the Yangtze River, accompanied by artists to make sketches, out of his desire to reproduce in the north the garden landscapes of southern China. He also commissioned European Jesuit architects, Sichelbarth and Benoist, to design Western buildings, including gazebos and follies, in an adventurous blending of West and East. The final result was three gardens: the Garden of Perfect Brightness, the Garden of Eternal Spring and the Garden of Beautiful Spring.

The Elgin masonry The broken masonry of the Old Summer Palace bears testimony to the destructive visit of British and French troops during the Second Opium War. In 1860, Lord Elgin ordered the site burned after his soldiers had thoroughly looted the place—some of their plunder may be seen in the British Museum and the Louvre. Today, there are ambitious, commercially motivated plans to restore the entire site. Opposing the project are those who argue the ruins should stand as a historical record of past injustices.

HIGHLIGHTS

- Museum with models and drawings giving some idea of the pre-1860 splendor
- Restored concrete maze to the west of the fountain ruins
- Tranquil picnic places away from the metropolis

INFORMATION

- ✛ Off the map, about 1¼ miles east of the Summer Palace
- ✉ Qinghua Xilu, Haidian District
- ☎ 6255 1488
- 🕐 7–7
- Ⓜ Xizhimen
- 🚍 375 minibus from Xizhimen subway station
- 💰 Inexpensive
- ↔ Summer Palace (➤ 24)

Below: Part of the 10,000 Flowers Maze

3

GREAT BELL TEMPLE

This unique little museum is in a Buddhist temple where you will see the Yongle Bell, the largest in China. A visit here is a rewarding experience, and the music of the temple's Bell Orchestra is a surprising pleasure.

The technology The temple-museum is home to hundreds of bronze bells from all over China, but pride of place rests with a 46.5-ton giant bell cast in the Ming dynasty known as the Yongle bell. It hangs on a huge wooden frame by a one-yard-long iron and steel nail coated with copper. The nail is 2 inches wide and pierces two U-shaped hooks around the wooden block. It is calculated that each 3/100 square inch of the nail can withstand 5¼ pounds of shearing stress. Displays in the temple-museum (in English) explain the technology of bell-casting in China.

Ring the bells You can get into the spirit of bell-ringing by thumping a large one outside the temple with the help of a small battering ram. Inside the temple, for a nominal fee, you can dip your hand into a large bowl of water before ferociously rubbing its twin handles to produce a musical vibration. If a certain frequency is attained, the vibrations cause spurts of water to appear—thus the bowl's nickname "Dragon Fountain." A narrow staircase leads to a platform above the giant Yongle bell, where an interesting wall display is devoted to the bell's history. The music of the Giant Bell Orchestra may be purchased in CD or cassette form. (If you decide to buy one, play it on the temple's music system, before departing, to make sure that your copy works.)

Fine design featuring bells, of course

The Great Wall

President Nixon exclaimed to his Secretary of State, "I think you would have to agree, Mr. Secretary, that this is a great wall." On some days the crowds of visitors also make it a great tourist circus.

Significance Mao Zedong said that anyone wishing to be a hero must first climb the wall, and for many Chinese people, the wall remains very much a part of their cultural identity. It was built between the 5th century BC and the 16th century AD; its purpose was protective although it served also as a military communications route. From the 17th century onwards it was left to crumble away, a process that was speeded by neighboring peasants seeking building material.

Symbol of cruelty At odds with its contemporary significance, the building of the wall was often associated with acts of great cruelty. Emperors like Qin Shi Huang in the 3rd century BC became infamous for their mobilization of enforced labor, and there are stories of sections being made with the blood and bones of their builders.

Practicalities Ask a few questions before settling for one of the many available tours. Which part of the wall does the tour visit? Badaling, restored in the 1950s, is the most popular location but, be warned, the commercialism and crowds may disillusion you. A cable car helps the large number of visitors. Simatai requires a degree of fitness and fortitude, as sections of the unrestored wall are unprotected at the sides. Mutianyu is accessible and safe and, like Badaling, offers a cable-car ride up and down the side of the mountain. Where else does the tour go? Check how much time is spent at the wall, and beware of time-consuming and often unrewarding trips to factory stores along the way.

DID YOU KNOW?

- The wall is the only human-made structure discernible from the moon
- The wall's bricks could encircle the earth in a 5½ yard-high wall
- Genghis Khan is said to have conquered the wall by simply bribing the sentries

INFORMATION

- ✚ Off the map to the northwest of the city
- ✉ Badaling in Yanqing County; Mutianyu in Huairou County; Simatai in Miyun County
- ☎ Badaling 6912 1235; Mutianyu 6964 2022; Simatai 6993 1095
- ◉ Badaling Mon–Fri 6AM–6:30PM, Sat–Sun 6AM–10PM; Mutianyu 6:30AM–6PM; Simatai 8–5
- 🍴 Restaurants and teashops (S–SS) at Badaling and Mutianyu
- 🚌 Tourist buses 1, 2, 3 from Qianmen terminal for Badaling; minibuses from Dongzhimen bus station for Mutianyu. No convenient access to Simatai by bus
- 🚉 Qinglongqiao
- ♿ None
- 💲 Moderate
- ↔ Ming Tombs (➤ 28) usually included in tours to Badaling or Mutianyu
- ❓ Hotels organize tours but prices vary; more expensive hotels tend to charge more

27

5

MING TOMBS

HIGHLIGHTS

- The mythological xiechi, a cat-like creature with horns, one of the six pairs of animals lining the Spirit Way
- The original, unpainted pillars supporting the Palace of Sacrificing, made from entire trunks of the nanmu tree
- Jewelry on show in the Palace of Sacrificing
- The royal treasures from Dingling found when the tomb was excavated

INFORMATION

- ✠ Off the map
- ✉ Shisanling, Changping County
- ☎ 6976 1424
- ⏲ 7:30–6
- 🍴 Most tours include lunch, at the Friendship Store (S–SS)
- 🚌 Tourist buses 1, 2, 3, 4, 5
- ♿ None
- 💰 Moderate
- ↔ Great Wall (➤ 27) usually included in tours to the Ming Tombs

Below: the main pavilion of the Ming Tombs

Willows whisper in the wind as the stone-carved figures along the Spirit Way stare imperiously at visitors following in the footsteps of the 17th-century mourners who carried the coffins of emperors to their final resting place.

Death of an emperor Of the 17 emperors who ruled during the Ming dynasty (1368–1644), 13 were ceremoniously laid to rest in this beautiful place about 30 miles northwest of their capital. The site was chosen for its geomantic qualities—facing Beijing, with mountains on three sides. Elaborate rites dictated the stages of the funeral. The deceased's concubines were also buried alive to comfort the emperor in the next world.

Not to miss The ceremonial avenue leading to the tombs, the Spirit Way, provides a wonderful opportunity to admire 18th-century Ming sculptures in their original context. Only three of the tombs are open to the public. At the end of the avenue, one of them, Changling, comes into view. Emperor Yongle was interred here in 1424, and the focus of interest at this tomb is the imposing Palace of Sacrificing and its collection of imperial riches. A useful model of the whole site is on show and the exhibits carry descriptions in English. At the rear of the palace, there is a stele tower, while an undistinguished mound behind railings at the back marks the actual burial ground. Of the other two tombs, only the excavated Dingling is worth a visit. A staircase leads to the burial vault holding a replica of the excavated coffin. In the courtyard, relics of the emperor and his two empresses are on display.

BEIHAI PARK

Kublai Khan is reputed to have created this popular park, Beijing's largest. Half water and half land, it offers a placid charm and an opportunity to relax in the city, if you avoid weekends.

History The lake in the park was dug during the Jin dynasty (12th–13th century), before the Forbidden City was thought of. All that remains of Kublai Khan's presence is a large, decorated jade vessel that was presented to him in 1265. It is now on show in the Round City, just inside the south entrance to the Park on Wenjin Jie. During the Qing dynasty, Emperor Qianlong (1736–95) directed an ambitious landscaping project that laid the foundations for an exemplary Chinese classical garden. Jiang Qing, widow of Mao Zedong and a 20th-century empress of sorts, was a regular visitor during the 1980s.

What to see Inside the south gate is the Round City comprising a pavilion and courtyard. Beyond, the Hall of Receiving Light was originally a superior gatepost house for emperors and is now home to a Buddha crafted out of white jade, a present from Myanmar to Empress Dowager Cixi, who ruled from 1861 to 1908. From the hall, the way leads to a short walk across the lake to Jade Island, noted for the White Dagoba, a 39½ yard-high Buddhist shrine constructed in 1651 for a visit to Beijing by the Dalai Lama of Tibet. Also here is the famous Fangshan restaurant, serving favourite imperial dishes, and a dock where you can rent rowboats. Off the island, the north shore has other places of interest (► Highlights panel).

HIGHLIGHTS

- The White Dagoba on Jade Island
- Elaborate, imperial-style Fangshan restaurant (► 62)
- Dragon Screen, on the north shore of the lake
- 17th-century Five Dragon Pavilions, near Dragon Screen
- Kublai Khan's jade vase, the largest of its kind in China
- Ice-skating or boating on the lake

INFORMATION

- ✠ F4/5, G4/5
- ✉ Wenjin Jie, Xicheng District
- ☎ 6404 0610
- 🕐 6AM–8PM
- 🍴 Snack and drink shops; Fangshan restaurant (► 62)
- 🚇 13, 101, 103, 107, 109, 111
- ♿ None
- 💲 Inexpensive
- ↔ Jingshan Park (► 30)

Detail from the Dragon Screen

7

JINGSHAN PARK

Get the best panoramic views of the Forbidden City's gold and russet roofscape from the top of the Pavilion of Everlasting Spring in Jingshan Park. Come here before visiting the Forbidden City and you will understand its vast scale.

History As far back as the Yuan dynasty (1279–1368), Jingshan Park was the private recreational preserve for the imperial family. In the 15th century, when the moat for the Forbidden City was being dug, the demands of *feng shui* dovetailed with engineers' need to remove tons of earth. By using this to create large mounds to the north of the imperial palace, the royal residence was able to be put on high ground and thereby protected from malignant spirits. A story circulated that one emperor kept coal under one of the artificial hills. Coal Hill is another name for Jingshan Park.

Reflection in a quiet corner of Jingshan Park

INFORMATION

- ✚ G5
- ✉ Jingshanqian Jie, Dongcheng District
- ☎ 6404 4071
- ◷ 6AM–9PM
- 🚌 101, 103
- ♿ None
- 🖐 Inexpensive

Vantage point In addition to the compelling sight of the Forbidden City, the central pavilion—perched on the highest point in the park easily reached from the park's main entrance—also takes in views of the long lake in Beihai Park and its White Dagoba (▶ 29). On a clear day, it is possible to see the Western Mountains to the northwest. The perspective of the city as a whole reveals how remarkably flat most of Beijing is, and it is easy to imagine the force of the biting winter winds scudding across the city.

Entertainment Back at the bottom you may catch a glimpse of a troupe of players dancing and cavorting as they lead a re-creation of an imperial procession, with the "empress" in her sedan, to the sound of court music.

8

FORBIDDEN CITY (PALACE MUSEUM)

Wander off the beaten track here and imagine the past: Emperors and empresses, concubines and eunuchs, court intrigues and decrees, palanquins, palaces and thrones. Make no mistake, this was the imperial heart of the Chinese civilization.

Architecture No other complex in the world can match the Forbidden City in its harmonious mix of monumental scale, fine detail, and geometry. For nearly 500 years (1420–1911) it was the residence and court of the Ming and Qing dynasties; today it is a museum complex, properly known by Chinese authorities as the Palace Museum, involving several major sites—official buildings, former residential complexes, imposing gates and gardens—that are visitor must-sees in their own right. Begin a tour at the main entrance, the Meridian Gate (▶ 51), through the 11-yard wall that surrounds the complex with majestic watchtowers on its four corners. The wall itself is surrounded by a moat more than 55 yards across.

All the main buildings in the Forbidden City are laid out on a north–south axis, starting from the south with the Halls of Supreme Harmony (Taihe) (▶ 36), Middle Harmony (Zhonge) (▶ 35) and Preserving Harmony (Baohe) (▶ 34). The Gate of Heavenly Purity (▶ 50) separates these official buildings from the residential quarter, the focal points of which are the Palace of Heavenly Purity (Qianqing Palace) (▶ 33) and the Palace of Earthly Tranquillity (▶ 33). Behind the royal bedrooms lies the Imperial Garden (▶ 32), which leads on to the northern exit.

Elitism Ordinary Chinese were barred from entering—hence the unofficial epithet. Most male employees were castrated but many volunteered for the honor of working for the emperor.

DID YOU KNOW?

- The Forbidden City is the largest palace complex in the world
- There are 9,999 rooms (10,000 would have been hubris)
- Its construction required 100,000 craftsmen and one million laborers
- The Forbidden City was declared a World Heritage Site in 1987
- On average, more than 10,000 people a day come to see the complex
- Many of the finest treasures from here have been in Taiwan since 1949

INFORMATION

- ✚ G5/6
- ✉ Xichang'an Jie, Dongcheng District
- ☎ 6513 2255
- 🕐 8:30–3:30
- 🍴 Snack shop (S) in the Imperial Garden
- 🚇 Qianmen
- 🚌 1, 4, 10, 22, 203
- ♿ None
- 💲 Moderate
- ↔ Many places of interest are in, or close to, the Forbidden City (▶ 30–6, 50–1)
- ❓ Taped guided tours in various languages can be rented at the southern entrance and returned at the northern exit.

9

IMPERIAL GARDEN (YU HUA GARDEN)

HIGHLIGHTS

- Rock garden
- Exhibition halls to the east of the garden
- Top of the north wall and view of Jingshan Park

INFORMATION

- ✚ G5
- ✉ Forbidden City
- ◷ 8:30–3:30
- 🚇 Qianmen
- 🚌 1, 4, 10, 22, 203
- ♿ None
- 🎫 Included in admission fee to Forbidden City

A post-modern display in the highly classical Imperial Gardens

A classic traditional Chinese garden: Trees and water in harmony; a rock garden and temples. Refreshments here are served in the "Lodge for the Proper Places and Cultivation of Things."

An imperial retreat There are four gardens within the Forbidden City but this one—some 100 yards by 145 yards—is the largest and most impressive. The arrangement of walkways, jade benches, pavilions and ponds was laid out during the Ming dynasty and, despite the fact that there are 20 buildings dotted around the place, the overall impression is of a relaxing natural setting. The imperial family had the Summer Palace (➤ 24) and other rural resorts to retreat to *en masse*, but the Imperial Garden (Yu Hua Yuan Garden), at the north end of the Forbidden City, was more readily available.

Repose The artificial rock garden arrangement, with a charming little temple perched on the summit, is one of the garden's most picturesque aspects. The large bronze elephants, with their faded gilt, contribute to an air of antiquity that is maintained by the centuries-old cypresses, which look as if they are close to the end of their natural lives. Surrounding bamboo plants are readily recognized but there are also other, rarer, plants in some of the flower beds.

Most visitors are justifiably weary by the time they reach the northern end of the Forbidden City, so try to allow time to rest in the garden for a drink or a picnic if you can. An old lodge dispenses snacks, clean toilets are available, and there are some reasonably interesting tourist stores on the east side (➤ 72).

PALACE OF HEAVENLY PURITY

Stories of passion and family intrigue have doubtlessly unfolded in this residential complex (also known as Quianqing Palace), in the private bedrooms of the emperors and empresses: In 1542 a maid nearly strangled Emperor Jiajing here.

Emperors at home Beyond the Gate of Heavenly Purity (▶ 50) lay the more private world of the Forbidden City, where the emperor lived with his family. The Palace of Heavenly Purity, during the Ming dynasty, was reserved as the bedroom of the emperor himself—the empress had her own quarters in the adjacent Palace of Earthly Tranquillity. The Qing dynasty preferred a less formal arrangement. Royalty lived in other rooms to the east and west of the main buildings, but the formal significance of the Palace of Heavenly Purity was not lost. When a Qing emperor died, his body was always placed in the Palace for a few days to signify he had lived a good life and had died while sleeping in his own bedroom. The successor to the throne was always announced from the Palace of Heavenly Purity.

Palace of Earthly Tranquillity This was the place for the consummation of royal marriages where the newly married emperor would spend the first days with his wife. The last emperor, Puyi, who came to the room in 1922 on his wedding night as a young teenager, reported as follows: "The bride sat down on her bed, her head bent down. I looked around me and saw that everything was red: Red bed-curtains, red pillows, a red dress, a red skirt, red flowers, and a red face... it all looked like a melted red wax candle. I did not know whether to stand or sit, decided I preferred the Hall of Mental Cultivation, and went back there."

The imperial boudoir

HIGHLIGHTS

- Hall of Mental Cultivation (west of Palace of Heavenly Purity) (▶ 50)
- Exhibition halls and museums of imperial treasures (east of Palace of Earthly Tranquillity)

INFORMATION

- ✚ G5
- ✉ Forbidden City
- 🕐 8:30–3:30
- 🚇 Qianmen
- 🚌 1, 4, 10, 22, 203
- ♿ None
- 🎫 Included in admission fee to Forbidden City
- ↔ Many nearby places of interest (▶ 30–6, 50–1)

HALL OF PRESERVING HARMONY

HIGHLIGHTS

- Dragon Walk
- Marble Terrace
- Archeological finds from the site, on display inside the hall
- Archery Pavilion (to the east of the hall)

INFORMATION

- ✚ G5
- ✉ Forbidden City
- ⏰ 8:30–3:30
- Ⓠ Qianmen
- 🚌 1, 4, 10, 22, 203
- ♿ None
- 🎫 Included in admission fee to Forbidden City

The solid marble Dragon Walk

When you see the remarkable marble Dragon Walk at the rear of this hall, the story of how it got there is a graphic reminder of what the designers and builders of the Forbidden City achieved—and all without the aid of machinery.

Banquets and examinations The Hall of Preserving Harmony (Baohe Hall) is one of the Forbidden City's three great halls. Behind it, to the north, the Gate of Heavenly Purity (► 50) marks the division between the official, ceremonial sector to the south and the more private residential area to the north. At first, the Hall of Preserving Harmony was reserved for the royal banquets that usually concluded major ceremonial events. Later, during the rule of Emperor Yongzheng (1723–35) in the Qing dynasty, the notoriously difficult higher-level imperial examinations were held here. Successful candidates were assured of promotion to top-rank bureaucratic positions, so competition was intense.

Dragon Walk Directly behind the hall, a broad marble walkway leads down from the terrace and forms the middle of a set of steps. It is known as the Dragon Walk: A design motif depicts nine dragons flying above swirling clouds. Some 10,000 men were needed to excavate the marble; to transport the 250-ton block the 31 miles from its quarry, wells were dug along the route to provide water, which was poured along the road and which formed a carpet of ice, since it was winter at the time. The marble block was pulled along this ice track, it is said, by up to 1,000 horses tied together.

HALL OF MIDDLE HARMONY

Imperial architects used open space to enhance buildings. A perfect example is the Hall of Middle Harmony, or Zhonghe Hall—a companion to the Hall of Supreme Harmony—best viewed by standing on the marble terracing some distance away.

Imperial dressing-room Of the three main halls aligned on the north–south axis of the Forbidden City, this is the smallest. It generally functioned as an all-purpose imperial hall. It was here that the emperor would be decked out in his fine regalia before proceeding due south to whatever important ceremony or event was taking place in the Hall of Supreme Harmony. Some relatively minor court procedures, such as the formal inspection of seeds before planting, would take place in the Hall of Middle Harmony. It was also where the emperor held audiences with high-ranking court officials or influential foreigners, and where dress rehearsals for various court rituals took place.

A smaller scale The Hall of Middle Harmony is not just a smaller version of the other two halls—it has its own unique features. First constructed in 1420, it was rebuilt in 1627 and the roof design, topped by a ball in its center, is different but has the same overhanging eaves with decorative figures along the end of each ridge. The smaller size of this hall allows you to take in the harmonies of its proportions, without being overawed by the scale. The interior has a carpeted platform and a large, yellow, cushioned seat which was reserved for the emperor. The interior columns are not as richly embellished as those in the other two halls, but the small squares that make up the ceiling are finely decorated.

DID YOU KNOW?

- The costume and regalia donned by the emperor varied for every event and were all laid down in regulations. Even the everyday gowns varied according to the day of the month—a black-and-white one inlaid with fur for the 19th day of the first lunar month and a sable one for the first day of the 11th month

INFORMATION

- ✚ G5
- ✉ Forbidden City
- 🕐 8:30–3:30
- 🚇 Qianmen
- 🚌 1, 4, 10, 22, 203
- ♿ None
- 💴 Included in admission fee to Forbidden City
- ↔ Many nearby places of interest (➤ 30–6, 50–1)

HALL OF SUPREME HARMONY

HIGHLIGHTS

- The ornate coffered ceiling
- Richly decorated columns, carved with gold foil dragons
- The Dragon Throne and the nine-dragon screen behind it

INFORMATION

- G6
- Forbidden City
- 8:30–3:30
- Qianmen
- 1, 4, 10, 22, 203
- Included in admission fee to Forbidden City

Smoke wafted from the mouth of turtle-shaped incense -burners

Here, the entire court population, many thousands in number, would wait in silence in the flagstoned area as the emperor ascended to his throne, then ritually kowtow nine times, as the eunuch choir rejoiced in song.

Supreme indeed Inside the Forbidden City, beyond the Meridian Gate (▶ 51), a courtyard leads to the Gate of Supreme Harmony and a stream crossed by five marble bridges. Two imposing bronze lions stand guard, the male holding an orb in his paw and the female a cub, a symbol of power and longevity. The vast courtyard ahead is dominated by the grandest single building in the Forbidden City, the Hall of Supreme Harmony or Taihe Hall. Here the robed emperor arrived in his yellow sedan chair to preside over important court ceremonies: Coronations, royal birthdays, the winter solstice and the New Year. In the marble courtyard stood the armed, personal bodyguards, ceremonially dressed in red satin suits, while members of the royal family filled the marble staircase.

Symbolism The Hall of Supreme Harmony stands majestically upon a three-tiered terrace, with its own small courtyard surrounded by a marble balustrade. The stairway is furnished with bronze incense burners and in the courtyard are further symbols of longevity, bronze tortoises and cranes that have a space inside for burning incense. A pile of grains on the west side of the terrace and a sundial on the east symbolize the power of justice that resided with the imperial government. Entry to the hall is prohibited, but the splendid interior may be viewed from the open doorway.

TIAN'ANMEN GATE

Imperial decrees were announced from the top of Tian'anmen Gate with dramatic aplomb—lowered in the beak of a gilded phoenix and received by dignitaries waiting on their knees.

Historic entrance When China was under imperial rule, the gate formed the first entrance to the Forbidden City and served as the ritually ordained point for the emperor's edicts. As such, it seemed an appropriate platform for Chairman Mao Zedong's announcement, on October 1, 1949, to the waiting crowd and to the world at large, that "the Chinese people have now stood up." Here, too, in the 1960s, Mao broadcast to the million-strong ranks of Red Guards that the time for a "cultural revolution" had arrived. A giant portrait of the Chairman hangs above the central portal (portraits of Mao are now rare in Beijing), with the slogan on its left reading "Long Live the People's Republic of China," and on the right "Long live the unity of the people of the world." In 1989, student protesters raised a giant statue of a woman holding a torch of democracy, the Goddess of Liberty, to face Mao's portrait.

City bridges The seven bridges spanning the stream in front of the gate were not open to all and sundry—only the emperor could use the central bridge.

Iconography Tian'anmen Gate has become a highly charged icon, not only for Beijing but for China as a nation. Its image is reproduced on everything from banknotes to tourist brochures. However, for the millions of Chinese who want to be photographed in front of it, the experience of being here is important, for its historical significance is deeply felt.

DID YOU KNOW?

- Chinese visitors like to rub the huge door knobs hoping that it will bring good luck
- For a less expensive rostrum view of Tian'anmen Square, use Zhengyangmen (Qianmen Gate ➤ 42)

PLA soldiers on duty at Tian'anmen Gate

INFORMATION

- ✚ G6
- ✉ Tian'anmen, Dongcheng District
- 🕗 8–5
- Ⓠ Qianmen
- 🚌 1, 4, 10, 22, 203
- ♿ Moderate (free to pass through)

15

TIAN'ANMEN SQUARE

The most momentous events in modern Chinese history have taken place here. The square still resonates uncomfortably with memories of the massacre of students in 1989, which gained it notoriety throughout the world.

A 20th-century gesture People had gathered outside Tian'anmen Gate since the mid-17th century —it was here that Beijingers assembled in 1949 to hear the declaration of the People's Republic. But because squares are not part of the vocabulary of traditional Chinese town planning, today's vast square, some 880 yards long by 550 yards wide, was not formally laid out until the 1950s, and it was then almost a political gesture towards a new vision of society. Subsequently, from 1966, vast rallies launched the Cultural Revolution from here, and in 1976 the deaths of Mao and Zhou Enlai brought millions of mourners to this spot. Then, for two months beginning in April, 1989, the square became the focus for the most serious threat to Party rule since its inception. In June 1989, the government sent in troops and tanks to bring the student protests to a violent end. No one knows how many died—hundreds for sure, possibly thousands.

Atmosphere Little prepares you for the experience of being in Tian'anmen Square. Its dimensions reduce everyone in it to disconcerting insignificance. Most Chinese visitors— tourists from every corner of the country—are as awestruck as foreigners by the colossal space and the cold, gray buildings on either side. The flying of a kite, music tinkling in the background and the taking of photographs add a touch of humanity. Try to be here late one evening, when a gentler mood pervades the lonely space.

Communism's red star atop a clock tower

HIGHLIGHTS

- Chairman Mao Memorial Hall (south) (► 41)
- Great Hall of the People (west) (► 39)
- Museum of the Chinese Revolution (east) (► 43)
- Monument to the People's Heroes (center) (► 40)

INFORMATION

- ✚ G7
- ◎ Qianmen
- ▣ 1, 4, 10, 22, 203
- ♿ None
- 🎟 Free
- ↔ Many places of interest are in, or close to, Tian'anmen Square (see "Highlights" above and ► 42, 53, 55)

GREAT HALL OF THE PEOPLE

Some of the troops firing on the students in Tian'anmen Square in 1989 are said to have appeared on the steps of the Great Hall of the People. They may have come via the secret tunnels built for the safety of the People's Congress in case it met at the time of a world crisis.

History The Great Hall of the People, occupying 656,200 sq. ft., takes up the west side of Tian'anmen Square. Barring a session of the People's Congress—which occurs only infrequently—the hall is open to the public. It was built in the late 1950s, and the monolithic architecture betrays its Stalinist origins. Margaret Thatcher tripped on the steps outside when visiting in 1982. In 1989 Gorbachev's entrance was blocked by ranks of demonstrators.

Sino-Soviet aesthetic The interior design is worth seeing as a definitive example of monumental scale seriously lacking in charm. The rooms are cavernous and forbiddingly gray in color and mood. From the Central Hall, stairs lead upwards to the assembly hall and the guest hall, fronted by a huge landscape painting brought alive by an ideologically red sun. There are some 30 reception rooms, each named after a region or city (including Taiwan) and decorated in a style appropriate to that area; some are open to public view. The Beijing Room is one of the most interesting, with three different-sized sets of chairs for the different ranks of those sitting on them. There is also an impressive mural of the Great Wall.

The way out of the Great Hall leads down to the basement, where uninspiring stores sell clothes and craft items.

DID YOU KNOW?

- The assembly hall, 82½ yards wide and 66 yards long, has just under 10,000 seats and 500 recessed lights in its ceiling
- The banquet hall seats 5,000 guests at a time
- Rooms in the Great Hall are sometimes rented out to foreign companies for conventions

INFORMATION

- ✚ G7
- ✉ West side of Tian'anmen Square, Dongcheng District
- ☎ 6605 6847
- ◷ 8:30–3:30
- Ⓠ Qianmen
- ▣ 1, 17
- ♿ None
- 🍴 Inexpensive

MONUMENT TO THE PEOPLE'S HEROES

The monument is charged with past dramas

This monument, the central point in Tian'anmen Square, is dedicated to all those who struggled for the glorious revolution. The site carries a warning to the effect that anyone trying to start another one will be sternly punished.

Heroes of the nation The foundations of the 41½ yard-high granite and marble obelisk were laid on the eve of October 1, 1949—the day that the establishment of the People's Republic was announced—but the monument was not officially unveiled to the public until 1958. The inscription on the north-facing side carries words of praise by Mao for all those who died struggling for the country's independence, "Eternal glory to the nation's heroes." A similar inscription on the south-facing wall carries the words of Zhou Enlai. The base of the monument is decorated with a series of bas-reliefs showing key scenes from China's revolutionary history. A graphic scene on the east-facing side shows Chinese people burning the opium that the British introduced into China in the 19th century.

No wreaths, please The two-tier platform upon which the obelisk stands is now closed off to the public and kept under guard—a sign indicates that any laying of wreaths or commemorative gestures is strictly outlawed. In 1976, after the death of the immensely popular Zhou Enlai, anti-government riots broke out when wreaths laid at the monument were removed. Again, in 1989, wreaths laid to commemorate the death of a liberal politician who had been sacked by the government became the catalyst for massive demonstrations that challenged the political order. On May 13 of that year, some 200 students pedalled to the square and launched a hunger strike around the monument.

CHAIRMAN MAO MEMORIAL HALL

Millions of ordinary Chinese still have a deep respect for Mao Zedong. A visit to his mausoleum makes this very obvious. Lines of Chinese citizens will wait for hours to file silently past Mao's preserved remains.

Exterior The Memorial Hall, behind the Monument to the People's Heroes at the south end of Tian'anmen Square, was completed in 1977 by volunteer labor, only one year after the death of the famous helmsman of the Chinese people. To date, it has seen some 110 million visitors. The inscription above the entrance, "Chairman Mao Mausoleum," was calligraphed by Hua Guofeng who succeeded Mao to the leadership of the Communist Party. The two-tiered structure is supported by 44 octagonal granite columns.

Interior Entry to the hallowed ground is through a vast anteroom dominated by a large white statue of Mao. The line of visitors moves forward inexorably into the main memorial hall where the embalmed body lies in a crystal coffin in a gloomy orange light, draped with the red flag of the Chinese Communist Party. It takes only a couple of minutes to file past the coffin. Photography is strictly forbidden. The mood is somber and reverent.

Technology The body is raised from its freezer each morning and descends after the last of the morning pilgrims. A number of apocryphal stories regarding the problems of maintaining the body gained credence when, in 1998, the mausoleum reopened after a nine-month "renovation"—looking the same as ever.

DID YOU KNOW?

- No other Chinese leader's body has been preserved; others have been interred
- The government overruled Mao's wish to be cremated
- 22 liters of formaldehyde went into Mao's corpse
- A dissident who publicly called for Mao's cremation in 1997 was exiled

INFORMATION

- ✚ G7
- ✉ South end of Tian'anmen Square, Dongcheng District
- ☎ 6513 2277
- 🕐 8–11:30 and 2–4 (closed PM on Tue, Thu and Sat)
- 🚇 Qianmen
- 🚍 1, 4, 10, 22, 203

An inspiring statue outside the mausoleum

19

QIANMEN GATE (ZHENGYANGMEN)

HIGHLIGHTS

The view from the top of the gate takes in:

- Chairman Mao Memorial Hall (immediately to the south) (➤ 41)
- Tian'anmen Square (to the south) (➤ 38)
- Great Hall of the People (west) (➤ 39)
- Museum of the Chinese Revolution (east) (➤ 43)

INFORMATION

- ✚ G7
- ✉ Tian'anmen Square, Dongcheng District
- 🕐 8:30–4
- 🚇 Qianmen
- 🚌 1, 17
- ♿ None
- ✋ Inexpensive

The entrance to the Gate is less forbidding than in imperial times

Emperors took their security seriously—a moat and wall ringed their private city and another large wall surrounded the inner city. All that remains of this is the large central portal of Zhengyangmen (or Qianmen Gate), which gives a sense of Tian'anmen Square's monumental scale.

History Entry into the Forbidden City was simply not an option for the general public; even access to the inner city was controlled by a series of nine guarded gates. On the south side of Beijing, Zhengyangmen was the main point of transit between the inner city and the residential areas outside.

The gate was constructed during the rule of Emperor Yongle in the first half of the 15th century. A sister gate (Jianlou) is clearly visible across the street to the south but, unlike Zhengyangmen, it is not open to the public. Originally, these two gates were joined by walls.

Visiting the gate When you stand with the Chairman Mao Memorial Hall behind you, the ticket booth is on the corner of the left side of the gate, while the entrance itself is on the east side. Inside, there are three levels. The first is a gallery of black-and-white photographs relating to Chinese history, with brief explanations in English. The second is filled with fairly uninspiring souvenir stores, and the third level has a more interesting store devoted to tea-drinking.

Picnics Outdoors are stone tables and Western take-out food is available across the street opposite Qianmen subway station.

MUSEUM OF THE CHINESE REVOLUTION

Half a day spent at this excellent museum representing the history of injustice and suffering in graphic detail will give you an easy introduction to modern Chinese history. Highly recommended.

History Architecturally a sister building to the Great Hall of the People, the Museum of the Chinese Revolution looms over the east side of Tian'anmen Square. The interior is far more fascinating than the exterior suggests.

Interior The Modern China Exhibition (1840–1949) on the ground floor is the focus for any visit. English translations with the exhibits give a crash course in modern Chinese history. A lot of the material is based around documents and enlarged photographs, which are usually well chosen and superbly rendered. Exhibitions cover the Opium Wars, the 1911 revolution, the foundation of the Communist Party in 1921, the Japanese invasion of 1937 and the war of resistance—all leading up to Mao Zedong's declaration of independence. Interestingly enough, after 1966, during the Cultural Revolution, the museum was closed but it is not clear why, as the contents conclude with the founding of the Republic in 1949. Until July 1, 1997, a giant digital clock outside the museum counted down the days, hours and seconds to the return of Hong Kong.

Don't get lost Note that its easy to confuse the museum's ticket booth and entrance with that of the Museum of Chinese History (▶ 55) which occupies half of the same building, so be alert on the way in so that you don't end up in the wrong place.

HIGHLIGHTS

- Photographs relating to the Opium Wars
- Exhibition room devoted to the Japanese invasion
- View from the window across Tian'anmen Square

INFORMATION

✛ H7
✉ East side of Tian'anmen Square, Dongcheng District
☎ 6526 3355
🕐 8:30–5 (last entry 4:15)
🚇 Qianmen
🚌 1, 4, 17, 57
💲 Inexpensive

A stimulating introduction to modern Chinese history

21

QINIAN HALL

Through the perfection and harmony of its proportions, this triple-roofed temple, the Hall of Prayer for Good Harvests, achieves a state of both ultra-modernism and sacred serenity. It represents the highest development of religious architecture in China and should not be missed.

The finest temple in Beijing

DID YOU KNOW?

- The trees used for the Dragon Fountain pillars were imported from Oregon
- The roof was built without nails or cement
- The number of tiles used exceeds 50,000

INFORMATION

- H9
- Tiantandong Lu, Chongwen District
- 6702 2617
- 6AM–8PM
- 6, 15, 17, 20, 35, 39, 43, 106
- Cobbled ramp at the west entrance to ground level
- Inexpensive
- Imperial Vault of Heaven (➤ 45), Beijing Natural History Museum (➤ 54)
- Audio-taped tours available

Tiantan Qinian Hall, or Hall of Prayer for Good Harvests is part of Tiantan, the Temple of Heaven, the largest group of temple buildings in China. Tiantan Park surrounds the temple off the north–south axis that aligns the major buildings in the Forbidden City. Ming and Qing emperors ceremoniously traveled the short journey south to Tiantan to offer sacrifices to heaven in springtime and at the winter solstice. Before the first Ming emperor made this sacred journey in the 15th century, this area was associated with religious rituals as far back as the Zhou dynasty (11th century BC–256 BC).

Qinian Hall First built in 1420 and completely restored in 1889 after a lightning strike, the hall was where the emperor prayed for a good harvest. It is an extraordinary structure—three stories and a three-tiered roof, with blue-glazed tiles, rising above marble terraces and seeming to float in the air.

The four central columns, the Dragon Fountain pillars, represent the four seasons, and the outer rings, of 12 columns each, represent the months of the year and the twelve divisions of the day or "watches." The complex artwork of the caisson ceiling, with a wood-sculptured dragon in the center, is best appreciated with binoculars. In the courtyard, south of the hall, one of the buildings has been converted into a large arts and crafts store.

IMPERIAL VAULT OF HEAVEN

Here, Ming emperors dressed in sacrificial robes, consulted their ancestors' tablets before ceremoniously ascending the steps of the Circular Mound Altar and performing rituals that had been refined over the centuries.

Wooden temple From the Gate of Prayer for Good Harvests, a raised walkway leads to the Imperial Vault of Heaven. Constructed entirely of wood, it is an octagonal vault with a double-eaved roof. Dating originally from 1530, it was rebuilt in the mid-17th century. In many respects it is a smaller version of the Qinian Hall, with a similar blue-tiled roof, to represent heaven, but it receives more light, so it's easier to appreciate the elegant art inside.

Echoes and more echoes Surrounding the Imperial Vault of Heaven is the Echo Wall, so-called because of its acoustic property, which allows two people standing next to it to converse at a distance. Additionally, in the courtyard, at the foot of the staircase, the first stone is said to generate one echo, the second stone two echoes, while a single clap or shout from the third stone produces three echoes.

Circular Mound Altar (Round Altar) This huge round altar, south of the Imperial Vault of Heaven, is not as impressive as the other build-ings of Tiantan, but its symbolism is highly charged and it is in fact the Altar of Heaven itself. The three marble tiers of the altar symbolize earth, man, and heaven and, accord-ing to Chinese cosmology, the central stone in the top tier marks the very center of the world. On the winter solstice, the emperor ascended to this spot and from a stone tablet read sacred prayers of indulgence.

Interior design is the highlight of the Imperial Vault of Heaven

HIGHLIGHTS

- Bridge of Vermilion Stairs leading to the Imperial Vault
- Coffered ceiling of the Imperial Vault, displaying a gilded dragon playing with a pearl
- Echo Wall and Echo Stones
- View of the Imperial Vault from the top tier of the Circular Mound Altar (Round Altar)

INFORMATION

- ✚ H10
- ✉ Tiantandong Lu, Chongwen District
- ☎ 6702 2617
- ◷ 6AM–8PM
- 🚍 6, 15, 17, 20, 35, 39, 43, 106
- ♿ None
- 🎟 Entrance charge included in ticket for Qinian Hall
- ↔ Qinian Hall (➤ 44), Beijing Natural History Museum (➤ 54)
- ❓ Audio-taped tours available

45

23

TEMPLE OF CONFUCIUS

HIGHLIGHTS

- 700-year-old cypress tree
- Hall of Great Achievements
- Steles in the courtyard

INFORMATION

- ✚ J2
- ✉ Guozijian Jie, Dongcheng District
- ☎ 6407 3593
- ⏰ 8:30–5
- 🚌 13, 113, 104, 108
- ♿ None
- 💰 Inexpensive
- ↔ Yonghegong (Lama Temple) (► 47)

Examination successes were recorded for posterity

Seek out this temple down an ancient hutong. Cooling cypresses in the courtyard lead to the tranquil temple with its commemorative arches over the doorway.

Confucius This noted philosopher and teacher (551–479 BC) taught the virtues of moderation, family piety and nobility of mind through good behavior. His conservative belief in the natural hierarchy of the ruler and subject won his ideology the favor of the emperors and, despite fierce criticism from the Communist Party, the influence of Confucius is still felt in Chinese society today.

Outside the temple Occupying the forecourt area are a number of cypress trees including an ancient one that is supposed to have been planted when the temple was built in the fourteenth century. The other notable feature is a collection of some 190 steles that record the names of candidates who, between 1416 and 1904, successfully passed the notoriously severe civil service examinations. Adjoining the temple stands the Imperial College, now called the Capital Library, where the emperor would deliver his annual lecture on classic Confucian texts. Stone tablets recording the texts are in a nearby courtyard of their own.

Inside The Temple of Confucius, built in 1302 and restored in 1411, does not contain any statues of the philosopher himself, but in the Hall of Great Achievements, the central altar contains a small wooden tablet dedicated to his memory. Emperors and high-ranking scholars came here to make offerings to the spirit of Confucius and conduct ancient rituals. Part of the temple is now the Capital Museum, housing an array of ritual implements used in the temple ceremonies.

LAMA TEMPLE (YONGHEGONG)

This is undoubtedly the liveliest functioning temple in Beijing—colorful and exciting, redolent of incense, and as popular with worshippers as with tourists.

Lama Temple's characteristic flamboyant eaves

From palace to lamasery Built in 1694, this was the residence of Yongzheng, a son of Emperor Kangxi, until 1723, when the son became the new emperor. Following imperial tradition, his former house was converted to a temple and in 1744 it became a lamasery—a monastery for Tibetan and Mongolian Buddhist monks. Closed down during the Cultural Revolution, but saved from destruction by deputy prime minister Zhou Enlai, the Lama Temple reopened in 1980 as a functioning monastery with monks from Mongolia. It has been suggested that the place is purely a showcase exercise in public relations, designed to demonstrate how the Chinese state tolerates Tibetan Buddhism. It has lovely gardens and a wonderful interior.

Layout The temple is a complex of halls and courtyards with a variety of interesting pavilions on either side. In the Hall of Celestial Kings, giant guardians flank a lovely buddha, who is smiling and rotund. The next hall, the Hall of Eternal Harmony, has three buddhas accompanied by 18 disciples. Beyond the next courtyard lie the Hall of Eternal Protection and the Hall of the Wheel of Law (the law being the cycle of death and rebirth). The final hall, the Wanfu Pavilion, contains a 25 yard-high buddha, carved in the mid-18th century from a single sandalwood tree from Tibet, and also flanked by guardians. A wonderful figure of a god with at least 30 hands is the focus of Esoteric Hall, on the temple's east side. One of two halls with the same name it was used as a place of scholarship for the study of scriptures.

HIGHLIGHTS

- Maitreya Buddha in the Wanfu Pavilion
- Hall of Eternal Harmony (Yonghedian)
- Prayer wheel in the Pavilion of Perpetual Peace (west of Wanfu)

INFORMATION

- ⊞ J2
- ✉ Yonghegong Dajie, Beixinqiao, Dongcheng District
- ☎ 6404 3769
- 🕐 9–4
- Ⓜ Yonghegong
- 🚌 13, 62, 116
- 💲 Inexpensive
- ↔ Temple of Confucius (▶ 46)   47

ANCIENT OBSERVATORY

HIGHLIGHTS

- 4,500-year-old pottery jar with pictographic solar patterns
- Star map from Song dynasty (13th century)
- Equatorial armilla of 1673
- Views of the city from the roof of the tower

INFORMATION

- ✚ K7
- ✉ 2 Dongbiaobei Hutong, Jianguomennei Dajie
- ☎ 6524 2202
- ◷ 9–11 and 1–4 (closed Mon and Tue)
- ◉ Jianguomen
- ▤ 1, 4, 9, 10, 43, 103, 403
- ♿ None
- ▣ Inexpensive

Explore centuries of Chinese astronomy through the range of star-gazing paraphernalia on display here in a corner tower of the city's walls with fine city views from the roof.

West meets East In the 13th century Kublai Khan founded an observatory near the present site, building on a Chinese tradition that was already well established. Islamic scientists were in charge in the early 17th century and when Jesuit missionaries arrived in Beijing, they astonished the court by their ability to make astronomical forecasts and soon found themselves in charge of the observatory. New instruments were installed, and the Jesuits remained until the early 19th century. In 1900, French and German troops stole many of the instruments; they were later returned.

What to see At ground level, on the other side of the entrance booth, a small open-air area displays reproductions of astronomical instruments. Also on ground level is a small museum with explanations (in English) of the main exhibits. These include a copy of the world's oldest astronomical account, a 14th-century record of a supernova. Steps lead up to the top of the tower, and on the roof there are eight original instruments—including a sextant, a theodolite, a quadrant and an altazimuth—most made in the 17th century. Back at ground level, the small rear garden contains more reproductions of celestial instruments as well as stone carvings recording constellations and solar eclipses. An interesting little store there sells small replicas of astronomical instruments, and just outside the main entrance is a jewelry store (▶ 72).

These original instruments were first installed by Jesuit missionaries

BEIJING's *best*

GATES & HALLS

Concubines and eunuchs

The majority of the thousands of inhabitants of the inner court of the Forbidden City were either concubines or eunuchs; most were recruited from the poor, and although a few became important and influential figures, the majority were little better than slaves. However, young men volunteered to become eunuchs because it was seen as an honor and at the height of the Ming dynasty there were some 25,000 court eunuchs.

A symbol of well-being and an assured future in China

> **See Top 25 sights for**
> **HALL OF PRESERVING HARMONY**
> **(BAOHE HALL) (► 34)**

ESOTERIC HALL

Of the two halls of this name in the Lama Temple, the more interesting is on the right (east) side as you walk through the temple from the entrance. It was once a place of scholarship for the study of scriptures. The focus of interest today is a wonderful figure of a god with a least 30 hands.

➕ J2 ✉ Yonghegong Dajie, Beixinqiao, Dongcheng District ☎ 6404 3769 ⏰ 8:30–4 🚇 Yonghegong 💷 Cheap

GATE OF HEAVENLY PURITY

The Gate of Heavenly Purity divides the official ceremonial buildings of the Forbidden City from the private inner court of residential rooms. During the Qing dynasty, state officials were sometimes granted an audience here with the emperor. Two gilded bronze lions sit before the gate, the female clutching an upturned cub, symbol of prosperity, in her paw while the male grips an orb, symbol of authority, in his claw.

➕ G5 ✉ Xichang'an Jie, Dongcheng District ☎ 6513 2255 ⏰ 8:30–5 🍴 Snack shop (S) in the Imperial Garden 🚇 Qianmen 💷 Moderate (included in entrance ticket to Forbidden City)

HALL OF MENTAL CULTIVATION (YANGXINDIANG)

One of the many private rooms on the west side of the northern half of the Forbidden City, this hall was home to Empress Dowager Cixi (► 12). It also used by the last emperor, Puyi, as a private bedroom.

➕ G5 ✉ Xichang'an Jie, Dongcheng District ☎ 6513 2255 ⏰ 8:30–5 🍴 Snack shop (S) in the Imperial Garden 🚇 Qianmen 💷 Moderate (included in entrance ticket to Forbidden City)

HALL OF UNION

Hall of Union standing between the Palace of Heavenly Purity (► 33) and the Palace of Earthly Tranquillity, is the middle of the three inner halls in the northern, residential area of the Forbidden City. During the Qing dynasty, it was used for royal birthdays and coronations. It now contains a set of imperial jade seals, a glockenspiel and an 18th-century clepsydra,

a time-measuring device worked by the flow of water.

➕ G5 ✉ Xichang'an Jie, Dongcheng District ☎ 6513 2255 🕐 8:30–5 🍴 Snack shop (S) in the Imperial Garden 🚇 Qianmen ♿ None 💵 Moderate (included in entrance ticket to Forbidden City)

MERIDIAN GATE (WUMEN)

This is the largest and most important of the four entrance gates to the Forbidden City. Only the emperor could normally use the central one of its five arched portals, but exceptions were made for the empress on her wedding day and also for the three candidates who gained the highest marks in each year's imperial examinations, who were allowed to use the gate once. From the Meridian Gate, the emperor would inspect his army, pass sentence on the captured troops of defeated armies, and present the New Year's calendar to his court officials. The present U-shaped, multi-eaved gate dates back to the 17th century when it was substantially restored.

➕ G6 ✉ Xichang'an Jie, Dongcheng District ☎ 6513 2255 🕐 8:30–5 🍴 Snack shop (S) in the Imperial Garden 🚇 Qianmen ♿ None 💵 Moderate (included in entrance ticket to Forbidden City)

SHENWU GATE

Shenwu (Gate of Spiritual Prowess) is the northern gate of the Forbidden City, built in 1420. Each morning, to announce the dawn, the bell was rung 108 times, followed by the drum. The procedure was repeated at dusk. Every three years, the girls selected as concubines used Shenwu to enter the palace. The tower, which gives good views across to Jingshan Park can be reached by a long ramp. It contains an exhibition related to the architecture of the Forbidden City (explanations in Chinese only).

➕ G5 ✉ Jingshanqian Jie, Dongcheng District ☎ 6513 2255 🕐 8:30–5 🍴 Snack shop (S) in the Imperial Garden 🚇 Qianmen ♿ None 💵 Moderate (included in entrance ticket to Forbidden City)

One of the five towers adding majesty to the Meridian Gate

Feng shui

Literally "wind and water," *feng shui* is the ancient Chinese system of geomancy that is used to determine the most propitious design and position for buildings. Today, *feng shui* experts are often consulted before the plans for a new building are finalized. They employ the same principles as those that governed the layout of the Forbidden City.

51

PARKS

An unusual pictorial display in the heart of Ritan Park

Tai chi

This form of spiritual exercise, sometimes known as "shadow boxing," is best appreciated when observed *en masse* in Beijing's public parks from around 6 to 8AM. It is particularly popular with older citizens and consists of slow, balletic movements of the limbs designed to balance the flow of energy (chi) through the body and attain a healthy spiritual poise.

See Top 25 Sights for
BEIHAI PARK (➤ 29)
JINGSHAN PARK (➤ 30)
OLD SUMMER PALACE (➤ 25)
SUMMER PALACE (➤ 24)
TIANTAN PARK (➤ 44)

DITAN PARK

Conveniently close to an underground station and the colorful Yonghegong (Lama Temple ➤ 47), Ditan (Temple of Earth) Park dates to the early 16th century when it was built for emperors to offer sacrifices to heaven. The original altar is now part of a small museum ($) which also displays an imperial sedan.

➕ J1/2 ✉ Andingmenwai Dajie, Dongcheng District ☎ 6421 4657
🕐 6AM–9PM 🚇 Yonghegong ♿ None 💷 Inexpensive

GRAND VIEW GARDENS (DAGUANYUAN PARK)

Laid out in the 1980s as part of a project to film the 18th-century classic Chinese novel *The Dream of the Red Mansion*, this is a pleasant place, away from the city center, with a strange artificial rock formation, a water pavilion and walkways around a lake. Readers of the novel may recognize some locations.

➕ C10 ✉ Nancaiyuan Jie, Xuanwu District ☎ 6351 8879
🕐 8:30–5:30 🚌 19, 59 ♿ None 💷 Inexpensive

RITAN PARK

Ritan (Temple of the Sun) Park developed out of a 16th-century altar site where the emperor made sacrificial offerings to the sun god. Situated in the heart of embassy-land, near the Friendship Store (➤ 72, 74) and the Russian market (➤ 74), it makes for a pleasant evening stroll (➤ 18).

➕ L6 ✉ Ritan Lu, Chaoyang District ☎ 6502 1743
🕐 6:30AM–8:30PM 🍴 Restaurant in northeast corner of park
🚌 1, 4, 9, 29, 48, 57, 103 ♿ Few 💷 Inexpensive

TAORANTING PARK

The first park here was laid out in the Liao period (947–1125) and during the Qing dynasty it became one of the few parks open to the public. Its swimming pool is a big draw with Chinese families, but there are quiet places to retreat to, including the remains of a monastery and a number of pavilions (this is also known as Joyous Pavilion Park).

✚ F10 ☒ Taiping Jie, Xuanwu District ⏰ 6AM–10PM 🚌 14 from Hepingmen underground station 🚻 None 💰 Inexpensive

TUANJIEHU PARK

This delightful little park, surrounded by high-rise office blocks and off the tourist trail, offers a relaxing diversion from palaces and stores. Paths lead through a scenic arrangement of lake, willow trees, humped bridge and greenery. There is a small amusement park with rides for toddlers.

✚ N5 ☒ Dongsanhuanbei Lu, Chaoyang District ☎ 6507 3603 ⏰ 6:30AM–9PM 🍴 Asian Star restaurant (► 66) 🚌 43, 115 🚻 Few 💰 Inexpensive

ZHONGSHAN PARK

This park, southwest of the Forbidden City, opened to the public in 1924, was later dedicated to Sun Yat Sen, leader of the 1911 revolution and the country's first president. In imperial times, it was the site of an altar, built in 1421 but still standing, where the emperor made twice-yearly sacrifices. Now, ancient cypresses shade locals and tourists alike and there is a children's play area.

✚ G6 ☒ 64 Xichang'an Jie, west of Tian'anmen Square, Dongcheng District ☎ 6605 5431 ⏰ 6:30AM–7PM Ⓠ Qianmen 🚻 None 💰 Inexpensive

ZIZHUYUAN PARK

Especially appealing, "Purple Bamboo Park" is famous for its abundant bamboo (whether there is any hint of purple in its color is debatable). One third of the 116 acres consists of lakes and rivers, and a variety of trees and shrubs insure delightful arboreal views.

✚ A2/3 ☒ Baishiqiao Lu, Haidian District ☎ 6842 0055 ⏰ 6AM–8PM 🍴 Restaurants (SS) at New Century Hotel (► 84) Ⓠ Xizhimen 🚻 Few 💰 Inexpensive

Youngsters enjoying a snack outdoors

Park life

In recent years, Western-style disco-dancing has become popular with middle-aged citizens as a form of exercise. Early in the morning they arrive with cassette players and even the occasional boom box, while alongside them more sedate movements are played out by tai chi devotees. Elderly men like to stroll with their bird-cages or sit and listen to the warbling of caged finches and orioles. Nearby, affectionate young couples enjoy the relative privacy of parks to neck on benches.

MUSEUMS AND GALLERIES

See Top 25 Sights for
FORBIDDEN CITY (▶ 31–6)
MING TOMBS (▶ 28)
MUSEUM OF THE CHINESE REVOLUTION (▶ 43)

Lu Xun

Hailed as the most progressive modern Chinese writer, Lu Xun (1881–1936), gave up a career in medicine to become a satirical writer. His most famous work, a short story, *The True Story of Ah Q*, is well worth reading. Copies in translation may be purchased at the Lu Xun Museum.

A bust of Lu Xun

Exhibits at the Natural History Museum

BEIJING ART MUSEUM OF STONE CARVINGS

On the site of the Wuta (Five-Pagoda) Temple (▶ 57), the museum contains 600 stone carvings from the Han, the late Qing dynasty. The explanatory text is not translated but sometimes an English-speaking guide is available. Rubbings of the stone-carved steles can be made. There is a collection of tombstones, some with Latin inscriptions recording the deaths of 17th-century Jesuit missionaries.

🔲 B2 ✉ 24 Wutasi, Baishiqiao, Haidian District ☎ 6217 2894/ 6218 6081 🕐 8:30–4 🍴 Nearby restaurant (▶ 62) 🚇 Xizhimen ♿ None 💷 Inexpensive

BEIJING NATURAL HISTORY MUSEUM

This place is very unique and strange. The ground floor, devoted to zoology, is by turns dull and kitschy, but upstairs, under the guise of anthropological study, there are displays of cross-sections of human cadavers and pickled organs. Come back another time if a school trip is in evidence.

🔲 G9 ✉ 126 Tianqiaonan Dajie, Chongwen District ☎ 6702 4431 🕐 8:30–5 (last ticket 4) 🍴 American-style fast-food outlet next door (S) 🚌 2, 25, 53, 59, 120, 803 ♿ None 💷 Inexpensive

CHINA ART GALLERY

Situated in one of the first big buildings to appear after 1949, this is the city's major art gallery and China's national art museum. Visiting international exhibitions (details in the *China Daily*) are held on the ground floor. Contemporary Chinese art is displayed upstairs. No socialist realism here; the subject matter is Chinese life, especially scenes of rural activity, and the

style is pictorial and mostly Western.
🏠 H5 ✉ 1 Wusi Dajie, Dongcheng District ☎ 6401 2252 🕐 Tue–Sun 9–4 🚌 103, 104, 109, 111, 112 🚹 None 💷 Inexpensive

FORMER RESIDENCE OF SOONG QING-LING

Soong Qing-Ling, the wife of Sun Yat Sen, lived in this former Qing mansion—home to the father of China's last emperor—from 1963 until her death in 1981. Quite apart from the exhibits relating to her life, the gardens are exquisite and worth a visit.
🏠 F2 ✉ 46 Houhaibeiyan, Xicheng District ☎ 6403 5858/ 6404 4205 🕐 9–4 🚌 5, 55 🚹 None 💷 Inexpensive

LU XUN MUSEUM

Situated next to the compound where the writer Lu Xun (► panel opposite) lived for a short time, the museum contains drawings with revolutionary themes, and material relating to his life and times, including the furniture of his study and bedroom. There are no explanations in English.
🏠 D4 ✉ 19 Gongmenkou 3 Tiao, Xicheng District ☎ 6616 4169 🕐 Tue–Sun 9–4 🚇 Fuchengmen 🚹 None 💷 Inexpensive

MILITARY MUSEUM

Dedicated to the history of the People's Liberation Army (PLA), this museum's graphic displays engage most visitors. The examples of Socialist Realist paintings and early photographs of Mao Zedong are especially interesting. Larger artefacts include a frigate armed with missiles and U.S. tanks captured in the Korean war.
🏠 A6 ✉ 9 Fuxing Lu, Haidian District ☎ 6851 4441 🕐 8:30–5 🚌 1, 4, 57 🚹 None 💷 Inexpensive

MUSEUM OF CHINESE HISTORY

Sharing a building with the Museum of the Chinese Revolution (► 43), the exhibits here become progressively more interesting as their coverage moves closer to modern times. Unfortunately, they are not explained in English. Check with the museum for special exhibitions.
🏠 H7 ✉ Tian'anmen Square, Dongcheng District ☎ 6512 8986 🕐 Tue–Sun 8:30–4:30 (last ticket 3:30) 🚇 Qianmen 🚹 None 💷 Inexpensive

XU BEIHONG MEMORIAL HALL

Relatively unknown in the West, Xu Beihong (1895–1953) is China's foremost modern artist. The galleries contain many of his paintings, including ones of galloping horses for which he is most famous. Reproductions are on sale in the museum store.
🏠 E2 ✉ 53 Xinjiekoubei Dajie, Xicheng District ☎ 6225 2265 🕐 Tue–Sun 9–12, 1–5 🚇 Jishuitan 🚹 None 💷 Inexpensive

Xu Beihong

The Shanghai artist Xu Beihong (1895–1953) experienced dreadful poverty after he was left as a teenager with the task of looking after his family when his father died. Later he traveled to France and became interested in the *avant-garde*, but he never lost his interest in depicting Chinese life, and his political radicalism insured his fame.

Xu Beihong is renowned for his paintings of horses

TEMPLES, CHURCHES & MOSQUES

See Top 25 Sights for
GREAT BELL TEMPLE (► 26)
IMPERIAL VAULT OF HEAVEN (► 45)
TEMPLE OF CONFUCIUS (► 46)
(LAMA TEMPLE) YONGHEGONG (► 47)

Religion

Taoism, Buddhism and Confucianism are the three main belief systems of Chinese religion. The government professes atheism and, while the freedom to practice religion is tolerated, there is strict control over places of worship (any new place of worship requires government approval), and contact with religious organizations outside China is not allowed. Mosques, Christian churches and Jewish Sabbath services also meet the needs of the city's worshippers.

BAIYUNGUAN TEMPLE

This Taoist temple, whose name means "White Cloud," dates back to the Tang dynasty. A factory during the Cultural Revolution, it has been restored and is now busy with Taoist priests and worshippers. The temple decorations include many familiar Taoist symbols like the Linghzi mushrooms, cranes and storks. A giant ancient coin on show is one of the highlights.

✚ C7 ☒ 6 Baiyunguan Jie, Xibianmenwai, Xuanwu District ☎ 6346 3887 ⏰ 8:30–4:30 🚇 Fuxingmen ♿ None 💷 Inexpensive

BEITANG (NORTHERN CATHEDRAL)

Built towards the end of the 19th century, the church—like many places of worship both Christian and non-Christian—was turned into a factory during the Cultural Revolution. Repair work was completed in the 1980s.

✚ F4/5 ☒ 33 Xishiku Dajie, Xicheng District ☎ 6617 5198 ⏰ Services in Chinese Mon–Sat 6–8AM, Sun 6–9:30AM and 6–7:30PM 🚍 38, 47 ♿ None

Above: the Fayuansi Temple

FAYUANSI TEMPLE

This delightful Buddhist temple, with its six lilac-decked courtyards, is now a college for novice monks, whose earnest, saffron-robed figures can be seen at their studies. The first temple on this site was founded in 645, and earlier buildings served many purposes, including that of an examination hall. Look for the display of illustrated moralizing texts on the right side as you go through the hallway leading to the main temple building.

✚ E9 ☒ 7 Fayuansiqian Jie, Xuanwu District ☎ 6353 4171 ⏰ 8:30–11, 2–4 (closed on Wed) 🚍 61, 109 ♿ None 💷 Inexpensive

GUANGJISI TEMPLE

A busy, functioning Buddhist temple redolent of incense, visited by a constant stream of devout worshippers. See it as part of a walk (► 16).

✚ E4/5 ☒ 25 Fuchengmennei Dajie, Xicheng District ☎ 6616 0907 ⏰ 8–4 🍴 ► 16 🚇 Fuchengmen ♿ None 💷 Free

NANTANG CATHEDRAL (SOUTHERN CATHEDRAL/ ST. MARY'S CHURCH)

Catholicism came to Beijing in the 17th century when Jesuit scholars were welcomed for their scientific, and specifically astronomical, knowledge. Nantang Cathedral is built on the spot where the most famous of these Jesuits, Matteo Ricci, lived.

✚ E7 ✉ Xuanwumendong Dajie, Xuanwu District ☎ 6602 5221 🕐 Services in Latin Mon–Fri 6AM, Sat 6:30AM, Sun 7AM; service in English Sun 10AM 🚇 Xuanwumen ♿ None

NIUJIE MOSQUE

The Chinese-style façade resembles that of a temple, but this is the largest mosque in Beijing—and the oldest founded in the late 10th century. Non-Muslims are allowed into the courtyard, but not the central prayer hall, where there are tombs of Muslim missionaries to China during the Yuan dynasty (1206–1368). The tower was used for observing the moon and calculating the time of Ramadan.

✚ D9 ✉ Niu Jie, Xuanwu District ☎ 6353 2564 🕐 8–5 🚌 6 ♿ None 💷 Inexpensive

WHITE DAGOBA (WHITE PAGODA) TEMPLE

It is not easy to miss this 50 yd-high pagoda, the largest in Beijing, built in the 13th century as a showpiece of the new Mongol capital. It was closed down and used as a factory in the Cultural Revolution. Nepalese influence in its construction is still apparent, and should survive the major renovation that was planned to be completed in 1999.

✚ D4 ✉ Fuchengmennei Dajie, Xicheng District ☎ 6616 0211 🕐 9–4:30 🚇 Fuchengmen ♿ None 💷 Inexpensive

WUTA (FIVE-PAGODA) TEMPLE

Established in the 15th century, this little-visited Indian-style temple and its adjoining Museum of Stone Carvings (► 54) are well worth combining with a trip to the zoo (► 60). Standing behind two ancient ginkgo trees, the temple's pagodas are covered with exquisite Buddhist bas-relief; climb the stairway for a closer view. After being looted by Anglo-French troops around the turn of this century, the temple fell into obscurity.

✚ B2 ✉ 24 Wutasicun, Haidian District ☎ 6217 3836 🕐 8:30–4:30 🍴 Nearby restaurant (Food St ► 62) 🚇 Xizhimen 💷 Inexpensive

Interior of South Cathedral

Islam in China

There are many mosques in the city and the Niujie Mosque is on the main street of Beijing's Muslim community. Islam was first introduced into China in the Tang dynasty (7th–10th centuries) and is now the religion of various minorities, including the Hui (from western China), some of whom live in Beijing.

White Dagoba in Beihai Park

AREAS TO EXPLORE ON FOOT

Pavement stalls in Dazhalan Jie

The first hamburger

The eastern corner of the south end of Wangfujing Dajie, where it meets Dongchang'an Jie (➕ H7), was the prestigious site of China's first McDonald's. In 1994 the government aired the notion of closing it down for redevelopment purposes. McDonald's resisted, and the media turned it into an international news story. Victory for the government? The fast-food restaurant has now closed down. Victory for McDonald's? There are now more than 30 franchised clones across the city.

BAIWANZHUANGXI LU

This street, south of the zoo (➤ 60), is the Beijing home to the Turkic Uighur (pronounced wee-gar) community, usually resident in northwestern China. Make a late evening visit when the restaurants and street stalls are open.

➕ A4 🍴 Shish kebabs, spicy mutton and nan bread (S) at most restaurants 🚇 Fuchengmen ♿ None

DAZHALAN JIE

Head south down Qianmen Dajie from Qianmen subway station and keep on the right side. After a string of stalls look for a blue-glassed building on the corner and "Billy's Shop" across the street. Turn right down the pedestrianized *hutong* (➤ 19) here. Down the first alley on the left is a centuries-old pickle shop, while back down Dazhalan Jie are musty old department stores with grand architectural façades, and an ancient medicine shop. Look on the right for the arched entrance (red lanterns outside) of a famous old fabric store. This is a side of Beijing that is fast disappearing.

➕ G8 🍴 Fast-food place at Zhengyangmen (Qianmen Gate) (S) 🚇 Qianmen

QIANMEN DAJIE

During imperial times, stores and places of entertainment for common people were not allowed inside the walls of the Forbidden City, so the area south of Zhengyangmen (Qianmen Gate) grew into a beehive of commercial activity, the legacy of which is still evident. It is especially popular with visitors from the provinces, and is an excellent area for foreign visitors to experience a colorful slice of Chinese street life. Qianmen Dajie, the main street running south from Qianmen Gate, bustles with working-class Beijingers. Attractions include a famous vegetarian restaurant, the Gongdelin, at No 158 (► 64); fascinating side streets like Dazhalan Jie (see opposite); and the Natural History Museum (► 54).

➕ G8 🍴 Fast-food places ($) and restaurants ($–$$)
🚇 Qianmen

SANLITUN LU

Don't miss this street in the northeast of the city, in an area populated by embassies. It has an almost Mediterranean character that's not Chinese at all. One side of the street is filled with clothing stalls (► 75), the other with alfresco restaurants. Black-market traders offer pirated computer and music CDs. Popular with locals, expatriates and tourists.

➕ M3 🍴 Plenty of cafés and restaurants ($–$$) 🚌 115, 118

XIDAN

The main thoroughfare that runs straight across the city from east to west changes its name four times and as Xichang'an Jie runs west from Tian'anmen Square before changing its name again to Fuxingmennei Dajie at Xidan. The Xidan area is worth exploring for its atmosphere, especially in the evenings when lively street stalls mushroom and crowds frantically shop for everyday household items.

➕ E6 ✉ Niu Jie, Xuanwu District
☎ 6353 2564 🕐 9–10PM
🚇 Xidan

WANGFUJING DAJIE

Once named Morrison St., after a London *Times* correspondent who lived at No. 88, this is one of Beijing's most famous streets. A large part of its eastern side has been extensively redeveloped as a showcase of modern Chinese consumerism (► 76), but it is still an interesting walk (► 18) and a good place to observe Beijing's *nouveaux riches* at play.

➕ H5/6 🍴 From fast food ($) to fine dining in hotels ($$–$$$)
🚌 104, 211

City Views

The Palace View bar, on the 10th floor of the Grand Hotel (➕ H6), is an excellent place for views of the Forbidden City. The transmission tower for Central China Television also provides a spectacular view of Beijing from 265 yards above the ground (➕ west of A5 ✉ 11 Xisanhuanzhong Lu ☎ 6843 7755, ext. 377 🍴 Restaurant and coffee shop at the top).

Beijing's popular Silk Market attracts locals as well as tourists

ATTRACTIONS FOR CHILDREN

See Top 25 Sights for
GREAT BELL TEMPLE (➤ 26)
SUMMER PALACE (➤ 24)
TIAN'ANMEN SQUARE (➤ 38)

Playgrounds

Most public parks have a playground suitable for toddlers and younger children and some of the mechanical contraptions are fun. Zizhuyuan (Purple Bamboo Park) (➤ 53) is good for rides; boat trips are also available. Older children might enjoy the video arcade in the basement of the Jing Guang Hotel (⊞ N5 ✉ Jing Guang Center, Hujialou, Chaoyang District).

BEIJING AMUSEMENT PARK

Here in the southwest of the city, on the west side of Longtan Lake Park, is an impressive range of fun rides—ferris wheel, roller-coaster, waterslide, boat rides and shooting arcades.

⊞ K10 ✉ Longtan Park, Chongwen District ☎ 6701 1155 ⏰ 9–6 🚌 60, 116 from Chongwenmen Dajie ♿ None 💰 Expensive

BEIJING ZOO

Fairly depressing by the standards of the great Western zoos, this one is worthwhile for its famous giant panda house—pandas being rare in the zoo world. Spare a moment for the lesser panda from Sichuan province. Tucked away northwest of the city, the zoo is easily reached by subway. A visit to the Museum of Stone Carvings (➤ 54) helps make the trip worthwhile.

⊞ B3 ✉ Xizhimenwai Dajie, Xicheng District ☎ 6831 4411 ⏰ 8:30–5:30 (avoid weekends) 🍴 Nearby restaurant (Food Street ➤ 62) 🚇 Xizhimen ♿ None 💰 Inexpensive

CHINA AVIATION MUSEUM

Military and civilian aircraft here include a twin-engined plane that Mao Zedong used for trips within China and the plane that flew over Tian'anmen Square on October 1, 1949. A separate building displays planes spanning the century.

⊞ Off the map ✉ Xiaotangshan, Changping County ☎ 6178 4882 ⏰ 8–5 🚌 912 from Andingmen subway station, 345 ♿ None 💰 Inexpensive

CHINESE ETHNIC CULTURE PARK

Though most Chinese are Han people, there are still over 50 minority ethnic groups. In this park near the Olympic Sports Center, exhibitions of architecture and the performing arts showcase the culture of diverse other groups. Wedding ceremonies, sports and song and dance performances also take place.

⊞ Off the map ✉ Corner of Fourth Ring Rd. and Beichen Lu ☎ 6206 3640/6206 3646 ⏰ 8:30–6PM 🍴 Food center in the park 🚌 380, 407 ♿ None 💰 Expensive

MOVIE TOURIST CITY

A genuine movie studio with sections set aside for visitors, including a horror set and children's games—the most popular game is laser tag.

⊞ Off the map ✉ Corner of Third Ring Rd. and Xitucheng ⏰ 9–4 🚌 302, 375, 367 ♿ None 💰 Moderate

Youngsters enjoy a ride at Longtan Amusement Park

BEIJING
where to...

NORTHERN CHINESE CUISINE

Prices

The restaurant descriptions use symbols to show approximate prices, for a meal for two excluding drinks, as follows:

$ under 100 yuan

$$ between 100 and 200 yuan

$$$ over 200 yuan

Northern cuisine

This category of Chinese food—taking in the whole area north of the Yangtze—includes imperial cuisine (reserved for, and specially prepared for, the court), Beijing duck and traditional city fare, along with food from remote northern areas like Mongolia and Dongbei. Noodles and steamed bread provide the basic sustenance, instead of rice, accompanied by vegetables and cold appetizers. From the far north come hearty beef and lamb dishes. Street cuisine is quick cooked food from mobile stalls with hotplates—pancakes filled with cooked vegetables are particularly delicious but it is wise to avoid meat fillings.

BANPO PRIMITIVE HOT POT BEER HUT ($–$$)

The primitive décor (bare walls and neolithic tools hanging from the ceiling) is a novelty—Banpo is the name of a neolithic village unearthed in the west of China. Spend an enjoyable evening tucking into the Mongolian hot pot meals, washed down by economically priced drinks. Very accessible.

✚ H5 ✉ 26 Wangfujing Dajie, Dongcheng District ☎ 6525 5583 🕒 11AM–1AM 🚌 103, 104, 108, 111

BEIJING EXPRESS ($)

An inexpensive place to enjoy northern Chinese street cuisine in comfortable and clean surroundings. The menu is divided into sections offering noodles, snacks, hot dishes and cold dishes—why not try a dish from each category? The noodle soup with double boiled spare ribs is recommended, as are the sautéed wild vegetables with shredded pork.

✚ A3 ✉ New Century Hotel, Shoudu Tiyuguannan, Haidian District ☎ 6849 2001 🕒 Lunch and dinner 🚇 Xizhimen

BIANYIFANG ROAST DUCK RESTAURANT ($$)

This famous roast duck restaurant has two dining areas, one pricier but also more pleasant, with more comfortable seats.

✚ J7 ✉ 2 Chongwenmenwai Dajie, Chongwen District ☎ 6712 0505 🕒 Lunch and dinner 🚇 Chongwenmen

FANGSHAN ($$$)

Court recipes once reserved for emperors' 19th-century meals form the basis of the elaborate imperial cuisine served at this renowned restaurant in Beihai Park. Sumptuous imperial-style surroundings.

✚ G5 ✉ Beihai Gongyuan (inside the east gate of Beihai Park) ☎ 6401 1879 🕒 Lunch and dinner 🚌 13, 101, 103, 107, 109, 111

FOOD ST ($–$$)

Situated behind the Xiyuan Hotel, close to the zoo, this is an excellent place to try northern Chinese cuisine at affordable prices. There are varied fresh fish dishes, noodles with shredded chicken, sweet dumplings, and delicacies like deep-fried scorpions. The barbecued meat cooked over charcoal and served on skewers is recommended.

✚ A3 ✉ Sanlihe Lu, Xicheng District ☎ 6831 3388 🕒 Lunch and dinner 🚇 Xizhimen

GOLD CAT JIAOZI CITY ($)

An English menu lists many tasty versions of stuffed dumplings—the specialty here. Dine outside in spring and summer for an altogether enjoyable experience.

✚ N5 ✉ Tuanjiehu Gongyuan East Gate, Chaoyang District ☎ 6598 5011 🕒 11AM–6AM 🚌 302, 402, 405, 801

LI FAMILY RESTAURANT ($$$)

The founder of this tiny and highly-regarded

restaurant was the great grand-daughter of an employee in the Qing court, who obtained the menus for Empress Dowager Cixi's meals. The restaurant, part of a family home, serves imperial dishes accompanied by a small number of Beijing and Li family dishes.

➕ F3 ✉ 11 Yangfang Hutong, Deshengmennei Dajie, Xicheng District ☎ 6618 0107 🕐 Dinner (reservations up to two weeks in advance are necessary) 🚇 Jishuitan

QUAN JUDE KAOYADIAN ($$–$$$)

The name means "old duck," but don't be put off—this is a fine place for a Beijing duck banquet (▶ panel). The restaurant has been in the same family for nearly 150 years and is now the flagship for a group of restaurants including a take-out outlet next door, that offers the same good quality dishes.

➕ G8 ✉ Qianmen Dajie, Chongwen District ☎ 6511 2418 🕐 Lunch and dinner 🚇 Qianmen

SI HE XUAN ($$)

Black-and-white photographs of old Beijing adorn the walls, in the spirit of the traditional cuisine of the city, in which this restaurant excels. Lunchtime is the best value, with cold appetizers like celery with tofu and hot dumplings, stuffed buns and noodles or congee (soupy rice); Chinese tea and pastries filled with lotus root complete a good meal.

➕ M7 ✉ Jinglun Hotel, 3 Jianguomenwai Dajie, Chaoyang District ☎ 6500 2266 🕐 Lunch and dinner 🚌 1, 4, 37, 52

TINGLIGUAN ($$)

Dining rooms of the Tingliguan ("Pavilion for Listening to the Orioles") surround a courtyard in the Summer Palace (▶ 24). You'll find a clever mix of imperial cuisine and Cantonese dishes that appeal to the Western palate. Try the fresh fish, including carp, from nearby Kunming Lake.

➕ Off the map 7½ miles northwest of the city center ✉ Yiheyuan, Haidian District ☎ 6288 1955 🕐 Lunch and dinner 🚌 301, 303, 332, 333, 346, 384, 904

TUAN JIE HU BEIJING ROAST DUCK ($$)

One of the most economical and visitor-friendly restaurants offering a good Peking duck. There are also lots of seafood dishes, as well as offerings that are less familiar to Western palates—like sautéed turtle.

➕ N5 ✉ Bldg. 3 Tuanjiehu Lu, Chaoyang District ☎ 6507 2892 🕐 Lunch and dinner 🚌 302, 402, 405, 801

Beijing duck...and more duck

Slices of roast duck are placed inside a thin pancake along with onion or cucumber and sometimes sweetened with plum sauce or a wheat jam. The taste is very rich and it is best not to think about the cholesterol count. A real feast begins with cold duck and ends with duck soup. A side plate of mashed garlic acts as an antidote to the rich, oily duck skin and meat.

Alcohol

Beer is available in most establishments in Beijing, but wine and spirits are likely to be found only in places patronized by tourists.

SOUTHERN & WESTERN CHINESE CUISINE

Southern cuisine

"Everything with legs except a table, everything in the air except an airplane and everything under the sea except a submarine." This Cantonese joke gives a fair idea of the variety of ingredients that go into southern cuisine. Fish— typically placed in a wok and lightly fried or, more usually, steamed— is a special favorite, as are the sweet and savory small plates that go by the name of *dim sum*, eaten for breakfast or lunch.

Sichuan

Outside China, Cantonese food may be the most widely known regional cuisine, but the western province of Sichuan provides the most surprises to the taste buds. The cunning use of spices, especially red chilli, gives Sichuan food a reputation for being very hot, but it is also very subtle. A typical appetizer might be fine slices of beef infused with the tangy peel of the kumquat.

AFANTI ($$)

Roasted lamb or chicken with nan bread are favorites at this conveniently located Muslim Uighur restaurant. Ethnic music and dancing in the evening make for an enjoyable night out.
✚ K5 ✉ 2 Houguaibang Hutong, Chaoyangmennei Dajie, Chaoyang District ☎ 6525 1071 🕐 11AM until the last customers leave 🚌 101, 110, 202

CHAIRMAN MAO'S FAMILY RESTAURANT ($$)

This restaurant is devoted to food from Hunan, Mao's province. Pork with bamboo shoots, a favorite dish of the Chairman, is always on the menu along with a number of typically hot dishes.
✚ J1 ✉ A4 Hepingli Zhongjie, Dongcheng District ☎ 6421 9340 🕐 Lunch and dinner 🚇 Yonghegong

CHAO YANG XIN JING ($$)

This Cantonese restaurant serves a range of seafood and, though well off the tourist track, has an English-language menu. In summer the outdoor tables are crowded with contented diners until the wee hours.
✚ Off the map, east of N6 ✉ 11 Hongmiao Lu, Chaoyang District ☎ 6502 3327 🕐 6AM–3AM 🚌 101, 112

DING TAI ZHEN ($)

The large menu in English features many fish dishes and old-fashioned western favorites like chicken rice with ginger,

as well as unusual appetizers like lotus root. This licensed restaurant is suitable for vegetarians. Try the Iron Fairy tea. Avoid the toilets!
✚ J5 ✉ 116 Dongsinan Dajie, Chaoyang District ☎ 6525 7578 🚌 110, 116, 120, 204

DYNASTY ($$–$$$)

Four dishes from the *dim sum* menu here make a good lunch for two; sautéed rice rolls, barbecued pork with raisins, deep-fried spring rolls, and dumplings with shark's fin soup are favorites. Ask which sauces go with each dish.
✚ N5 ✉ Jing Guang New World Hotel, Jing Guang Centre, Hujialou, Chaoyang District ☎ 6501 8888 🕐 Lunch and dinner 🚌 9, 113, 402, 405, 801

GONGDELIN ($$)

This is a branch of a famous Shanghai vegetarian restaurant, with its own delightful English-language menu featuring, for example, "chicken cutlets in the shape of lantern" and "the Fire is singeing the Snow-Capped Mountains." The food is excellent and the mock-meat dishes satisfy carnivores as well as vegetarians.
✚ G9 ✉ 158 Qianmen Dajie, Chongwen District ☎ 6511 2542 🕐 10:30–8:30PM 🚇 Qianmen

SICHUAN RESTAURANT ($$)

Overlooks the lobby of the Xiyuan Hotel. Be sure to try the Eight Treasures tea or the hotel's own strong brew of Kaiser beer. Spiced chicken is a fine cold appetizer and braised fish in black bean sauce a typical main course. The fried walnuts make a delicious dessert.

B3 ⊠ Xiyuan Hotel, 1 Sanlihe Lu, Haidian District ☎ 6831 3388 ⏰ Lunch and dinner 🚇 Xizhimen

SUI YUAN ($$$)

Superb Cantonese cuisine in the Beijing Hilton. Specialties change, but you can rely on the stir-fried fish dishes, and in winter the Mongolian-style chicken and beef satay is unbeatable. A Beijing duck set menu is available, and at lunchtime the shrimp dumplings and spring rolls are tempting. Live classical music at night.

N2 ⊠ Hilton Hotel, 1 Dongfang Lu, Dongsanhuanbei Lu, Chaoyang District ☎ 6466 2288 ⏰ Lunch and dinner 🚌 302, 402, 801

TIANSHI ($-$$)

Excellent and attractive vegetarian restaurant with mock meat dishes like deep fried chicken, rice with seafood, braised eel. Pictures of famous vegetarians— Shakespeare?—line the stairs. Superb non-alcoholic cocktails, beer and champagne. Snacks and soft drinks are served downstairs.

J5 ⊠ 57 Dengshikouxi Jie, Dongcheng District ☎ 6524 2349/6524 2476 ⏰ 8AM–midnight 🚌 108, 111

TIBET SHAMBALA ($)

The only Tibetan restaurant in Beijing (run by a Tibetan scholar) is well worth the rather long journey from the city center. Meals start with yak butter tea, and the dishes include wonderful noodles, barbecued lamb and a host of others with tastes that are unique to Tibetan cuisine.

A1 ⊠ 301 Minzu Shipin Yitiaojie. Weigongcun Lu, Haidian District ☎ 6842 2631 ⏰ Lunch and dinner 🚌 320, 337, 904

WISDOM BIRD ($-$$)

Don't be put off by menu items like stewed bullfrog; alternatives include spare ribs with bamboo shoots and interesting fish dishes. Few tourists find their way to this restaurant, tucked away some 220 yards down a lane and not named in English.

Off the map, just north of A1 ⊠ On the right side of a small lane leading off Baishiqiao Lu opposite the Friendship Hotel ☎ 6217 1941 ⏰ 11–10 🚇 Xizhimen

YU XIAN ($)

The chef and owner of this small restaurant was once Mao Zedong's chef; Mao's children and Deng Xiaoping have eaten here. The menu offers local items and traditional dishes from Hunan. Try the fish balls, or the meat-filled rolls that you put into little pancakes before eating them.

H5 ⊠ Cuihua Hutong, off Wangfujing Dajie, Dongcheng District ☎ 6524 5322 ⏰ Lunch and dinner 🚌 103, 104, 108, 111

Eight Treasures tea

A specialty of Sichuan restaurants is Eight Treasures tea, served out of the longest teapot you are ever likely to see. The eight ingredients are: Jasmine, jujule, walnut, fruit of Chinese wolfberry, raisin, crystal sherry, ginseng, and dried longan pulp. The taste is slightly spicy, and prepares you for the spicy flavors to come.

ASIAN RESTAURANTS

Asian food

Not so many years ago, the possibility of enjoying an authentic Indian or Thai meal in Beijing would have been unthinkable. Today, chefs are regularly brought in from other parts of Asia, and authentic pineapple fried rice, spicy Thai soup, nan bread, Masala tea and tandoori chicken offer exciting alternatives to Chinese food.

ASIAN STAR ($$)

Eclectic menu featuring Thai, Malaysian and Indonesian fare as well as a host of Indian ones—thanks to an Indian chef, options such as curries and tandoori chicken vie with the Malaysian dishes as some of the best Asian eating you will find in Beijing.

➕ N4 ✉ 26 Dongsanhuanbei Lu, Chaoyang District ☎ 65916716 🕐 Lunch and dinner 🚌 113, 402, 405

BOROM PIMAN ($$$)

The consensus among Beijing's expatriate community is that this restaurant in the Holiday Inn out on the road to the airport offers the best Thai food in the city. The service is exemplary and the décor Thai.

➕ Off the map near the airport ✉ Holiday Inn Lido, Jichang Lu, Jiangtai Lu, Chaoyang District ☎ 6437 6688 🕐 Lunch and dinner 🚌 401, 403

HEPINGMEN KOREAN BBQ ($–$$)

Korean restaurants in Beijing tend not to translate their menus, so non-Korean diners must rely on photographs or look around to see what is being served. The specialty is barbecued meats: a small grill is brought to the table for diners to do their own barbecuing. Good fun for newcomers to Korean cuisine as well as for old hands—but not for those who dislike hot, spicy food.

➕ G8 ✉ 15 Hepingmenwaidong Jjie,

Chongwen District ☎ 6301 3117 🕐 Lunch and dinner 🚇 Hepingmen

OMAR KHAYYAM ($$–$$$)

Authentic Indian cuisine for both vegetarians and meat-eaters. The menu is large enough to suit most tastes, and the lassi drinks are exellent. On weekends a reservation is recommended.

➕ L6 ✉ Asia Pacific Building, 8 Yabao Lu, Chaoyang District ☎ 6513 9988 🕐 Lunch and dinner 🚇 Jianguomen

RASA SAYANG ($$)

The best selection of basic Indonesian dishes in town.

➕ Off the map ✉ Holiday Inn Lido, Jichang Lu, Jiangtai Lu, Chaoyang District ☎ 6437 6688 🕐 Lunch and dinner 🚌 401, 403

RED BASIL ($$–$$$)

An excellent Thai restaurant. The superb food prepared by Thai chefs warrants the trip to the Third Ring Road just south of Sanyan Bridge. The menu does not indicate how spicy the various dishes are but the staff is helpful.

➕ N1 ✉ Building 8, Nanxiaojie, Sanyuanli, Chaoyang District ☎ 6460 2339 🕐 Lunch and dinner 🚌 302

SAIGON INN ($$$)

This restaurant in the Gloria Plaza Hotel serves traditional Vietnamese appetizers like *cha gio* and *goi cuon* (spring rolls), which you wrap up in lettuce and rice paper respectively. Tasty main dishes include chicken curry accompanied by shrimp salad, pickled vegetables and asparagus and crabmeat soup. The décor, right down to the chopsticks, is Vietnamese, and traditional Vietnamese music plays softly in the background.

✚ L7 ✉ 2 Jianguomenwai Dajie, Chaoyang District ☎ 6515 8855 ⏰ Lunch and dinner 🚇 Jianguomen

SANSI LANG ($–$$)

The most affordable Japanese restaurant in the city. Try the tempura and sushi. Although the menu is not in English, there are photographs of all the dishes.

✚ N2 ✉ 52 Liangmaqiao Lu, Chaoyang District ☎ 6464 5030 ⏰ 11–11 🚌 9, 300, 402, 801

SAWASDEE RESTAURANT ($$$)

A Thai restaurant offering dishes like spring rolls and *tom yam* soup, *galng ka-ree* (yellow chicken) curry with potatoes and *kaow ob sup-pa-ros* (fried rice with pineapple and seafood). Most dishes are quite mild, so this is a good place to try Thai food if you're wary of too much spice.

✚ J5 ✉ Song He Hotel, 88 Dengshixikou Dajie, Dongcheng District ☎ 6513 8822 ⏰ Lunch and dinner 🚌 104, 108

SHAMIANA ($$–$$$)

The first Indian restaurant to open in Beijing continues to provide quality meals prepared by an Indian chef. Some

dishes may seem bland to connoisseurs, but the chef will happily add more spice on request.

✚ D4 ✉ Holiday Inn Downtown, 98 Beilishi Lu, Xicheng District ☎ 6833 8822 ⏰ Lunch and dinner 🚇 Fuchengmen

SUSAN'S CAFÉ ($)

An unpretentious, friendly little place opposite the Kempinski Hotel. Meat and vegetable curries of varying degrees of spiciness are the main dishes, but soups and salads are also available. Cocktails are served (happy hour 3–6 daily).

✚ N2 ✉ Liangmaqiao Lu, Chaoyang District ☎ 6464 0930 ⏰ 11AM–2AM 🚌 9, 300, 402, 801

THAILAND EMPRESS SEAFOOD ($$)

Reasonably priced Thai establishment with an emphasis on seafood but a good range of other dishes as well. The menu carries explanations in English.

✚ F5 ✉ Xihuangchenggennan Jie, Xicheng District ☎ 6617 5754 ⏰ Lunch and dinner 🚌 22, 103

Quenching thirst

The Sawasdee Thai restaurant serves Guinness as well as other alcoholic drinks, but for many diners a bottle of cold mineral water, readily available in all Beijing restaurants, is a better complement to hot and spicy food. Best of all is a platter of fresh fruit, a lassi drink from India, or a glass of Thai iced coffee.

WESTERN RESTAURANTS

Dining with a view

On the 26th floor of the Xiyuan Hotel, the Carousel revolving restaurant serves Beijing and other Asian dishes (SSS) while taking in panoramic views of the city. The TV Tower (➤ 59) has a restaurant and café, but its view cannot match that of the Belle Vue restaurant on the 29th floor at the Kunlon Hotel (✚ N2 opposite the Lufthansa Center, ➤ 76), which takes about 90 minutes to complete one revolution.

BEIJING AUTUMN JADE ($$-$$$)

A mixed menu of French, German and Russian dishes—steak, chicken Kiev and pork chops, for example—served in an elegant setting by candlelight. Seafood dishes are also served.
✚ J6 ✉ 3 Jinyu Hutong, Dongcheng District ☎ 6512 8833 ⏰ Lunch and dinner 🚌 104, 106

CAFE KRANZLER ($$-$$$)

Situated on the ground floor of the Lufthansa Center, with tables looking out through oversized windows to the street, this comes to life in the evening, when live music helps provide a more relaxing atmosphere than might have seemed possible in this busy location. Steaks, pasta and pizza are on the menu.
✚ N2 ✉ Lufthansa Center, 50 Liangmaqiao Lu, Chaoyang District ☎ 6465 3388 ⏰ Lunch and dinner (closes 2AM) 🚌 9, 300, 402, 801

HOF BRAUHAUS ($$-$$$)

House specialties include Wiener schnitzel and smoked pork loin with sauerkraut and potatoes. The bonus is Hof Brauhaus' own beer, brewed using German technology. The menu is in English and German.
✚ N4 ✉ 15 Dongsanhuanbei Lu, Chaoyang District ☎ 6591 4598 ⏰ 11:30AM– midnight 🚌 113, 117, 801

LAXENOXEN ($$-$$$)

For fresh Norwegian salmon, you can't beat this Scandinavian restaurant in the Radisson SAS Hotel in the northeast of the city (➤ 84). Beef is regularly flown in, and the Sunday brunch is luxurious.
✚ Just north of M1 ✉ 6A Beisanhuandong Lu, Chaoyang District ☎ 6466 3388 ⏰ Lunch and dinner 🚌 302, 379

LE PETIT PARIS ($$)

A spacious French restaurant, complete with a reproduction of the bottom half of the Eiffel Tower, with a menu in French and English and a decent wine list. Crêpes here make a good lunch when you're shopping at nearby Sanlitun (➤ 75).
✚ M4 ✉ 8 Gongrentiyuchangbei Lu, Chaoyang District ☎ 6507 2228 ⏰ 11AM–midnight 🚌 113, 117

LOUIE'S SPACE ($)

A modest little café opposite the Kempinski Hotel, serving steaks, salads and sandwiches. Open until 2AM, happy hour from early afternoon until 8PM.
✚ N2 ✉ Liangmaqiao Lu, Chaoyang District ☎ 6462 1973 ⏰ 11AM–2AM 🚌 300, 402, 801

MEXICAN WAVE ($$-$$$)

Margaritas and beer imported from Mexico, make an appropriate prelude to the pizzas, quesadillas, burritos, burgers and huge salads. Near the corner of

Guanghua Lu.
🚑 M6 ✉ Dongdaqiao Lu, Chaoyang District ☎ 6506 3961 🕙 10AM–2AM 🚌 28, 403

MOSCOW ($–$$)

For decades after it opened in 1954, this Russian restaurant was prestigious. The reason to come here now is to dine surrounded by faded elegance, under chandeliers and amid fluted columns. While the spicy borscht is still worth ordering, some dishes can be disappointing. Try the steak with mushroom sauce or the chicken curry drumsticks.
🚑 C3 ✉ 135 Xizhimenwai Dajie, Xicheng District (access by a small road on the west side of the Beijing Exhibition Center; look for *Mockba Pectopah* about 110 yards down on the right) ☎ 6831 6677 ext.4331 🕙 Lunch and dinner 🚇 Xizhimen

POWER HOUSE ($$)

Photographs on the menu here offer standard items like spaghetti bolognese, pork chops and burgers. Live music at night keeps things lively. Close to the Sanlitun area.
🚑 N4 ✉ Gongrentiyuchangbei Lu (opposite the Zhao Long Hotel), Chaoyang District ☎ 6462 9192 🕙 10AM–2AM 🚌 113, 117

ROMA RISTORANTE ITALIANO ($$$)

Leather upholstery and wood paneling at this restaurant in the Palace Hotel (➤ 84) help create an elegant setting for dishes from northern Italy,

complemented by wines from a fine list. The set-price Sunday brunch offers a lavish choice of appetizers, pastas, soups, salads and desserts.
🚑 J6 ✉ Jinyu Hutong, Dongcheng District ☎ 6512 8899 🕙 Lunch and dinner 🚌 103, 104, 110, 116, 120

SYMPHONY ($$$)

The period European dining room here is elegant and luxurious, and the steaks and seafood are imported.
🚑 N2 ✉ Kempinski Hotel, Lufthansa Center, 50 Liangmaqiao Lu, Chaoyang District ☎ 6465 3388 🕙 Lunch and dinner 🚌 300, 402, 801

SZENARIO ($$–$$$)

At this delightfully informal Italian restaurant, start with the antipasto buffet, followed by pasta, pizza, salad or a grill.
🚑 L4 ✉ Swissotel (Hong Kong Macau Center), Dongsishi Tiao Lu, Chaoyang District ☎ 6501 2288 🕙 Lunch and dinner 🚇 Dongsishitao

TED'S CAFÉ ($$)

Places serving both Chinese and Western dishes are not common; the pub-like Ted's Café is an honorable exception. Typical European meals are served after 9PM while hotter Sichuan fare is available for lunch and for dinner between 6 and 9. Live music on weekends, organized games of darts every Thursday.
🚑 M6 ✉ 58 Guandongdiannan Jie, Chaoyang District ☎ 6506 0329 🕙 24 hours 🚌 9, 113, 402, 405, 801

Fast food

Nearly all major franchised fast-food restaurants are adding outlets in and around Beijing: A&W, Baskin Robbins, Dunkin' Donuts, KFC, McDonald's, Pizza Hut and TGI Friday's. A stretch of Jianguomenwai Dajie (L7), the area around Zhengyangmen (Qianmen Gate ➤ 42) and Wangfujing (➤ 59), are the places to find out how American fast food translates in a decidedly Chinese setting.

ANTIQUES

Exporting antiques

Chinese authorities classify any item made before 1949 as an antique. The export of any such item must be approved by the Beijing Cultural Relics Bureau. Approval takes the form of a red wax seal and an official receipt; any genuine antique dealer should be able to show you this. As the vast majority of "antiques" are really reproductions, the need for export approval does not arise very often. If you buy an antique that lacks the seal, you can have it verified and approved at the Friendship Store (☎ 6401 4608 for an appointment) every Monday afternoon. Packing and shipping are not generally available, and credit cards are accepted only at larger, modern stores.

BEIJING CURIO CITY

This large mall has over 200 stalls selling a wide range of items from bric-à-brac to genuine antiques. The best time to visit is on Sunday morning, when vendors set up shop in the surrounding streets.

➕ Off the map, southwest of the city ✉ Dongsanhuan Nan Lu, west of Huawei Bridge ☎ 6773 6098 ◷ 9–5

CHAOYANGMENWAI MARKET

Two large warehouses at the end of a small lane are stuffed with antique objects of desire: medicine cabinets, chests, first-class reproductions of Qing and Ming furniture, ceramics, Mao memorabilia, jewelry and other knick-knacks. A visit is vital for anyone thinking of buying a piece of furniture or a quality *objet d'art*. Packing and shipping are easily arranged. Serious bargaining is essential. Try to end up paying less than half the price first quoted.

➕ L5 ✉ Shichangie, Chaoyangmenwai Dajie, Chaoyang District ◷ 9–6 🚇 Chaoyangmen

HONGQIAO MARKET

Seek out the antique shops on the third floor—easy to miss, tucked away behind the pearl stalls (► 73). A lot of the merchandise is reproduction, but some of the furniture is small enough to be portable, and the temple plaques are appealing. Shop No. 6 specializes in old clocks. Bear in mind when bargaining that these stores sell primarily to tourists.

➕ J9 ✉ Tiantan Lu, Chongwen District ◷ 9–6 🚌 36, 39, 43

HUAXIA ARTS & CRAFTS BRANCH STORE

The second floor of this government store retails clocks, pocket watches, rugs, chinaware and woodcarvings from temples. Most of them are probably fake, but they look authentic.

➕ H6 ✉ 293 Wangfujing Dajie, Chaoyang District ☎ 6513 6204 ◷ 9–7

LIANGMAHE MARKET

In an arcade opposite the Kempinski Hotel, some 50 small stores sell pottery, paintings, old watches and antique furniture. One or two of the furniture dealers have a larger stock in their warehouses and will happily take potential customers there to view. However, there is a high mark-up, and you'll pay a reasonable price only after serious bargaining.

➕ N2 ✉ 49 Liangmaqiao Lu, Chaoyang District ☎ 6501 3525 ◷ 9–9 🚌 9, 300, 402, 801

LIULICHANG

Conveniently located southwest of Qianmen, this famous old street—now renovated to look its age—is well worth a visit even if you buy nothing. Fine antique stores stock woodblock print reproductions, porcelain, jade, snuff bottles, paintings and a very few genuine antique pieces. Worth considering are the rubbings of bas-relief carvings taken off ancient temples and tombs. A number of the larger stores are government-owned; bargaining in this area is limited.

➕ F8 ✉ Liulichangdong Jie, Xuanwu District 🕐 9–6 🚇 Qianmen

PANJIAYUAN MARKET

Come here early on weekends, especially Sundays; by afternoon this market is already winding down. Most of the "antiques" are fake, but they are quality fakes and gratifying purchases may be made if you bargain rigorously. Never pay anything like the first price quoted. It is best to arrive by taxi, but make sure the taxi driver doesn't just drop you by the stalls selling worthless bric-à-brac—ask your hotel to specify in writing that you want to go the antiques part of the market.

➕ M10 ✉ Huawei Lu Dajie, Dongsanhuan, Chaoyang District 🕐 8–1 🚌 35, 41

QIANMEN CARPET

Wares at this establishment are similar to those at Xu Cai Chun (below). There are some very expensive antique carpets from Xinjiang and Tibet as well as hand-made imitations and Henan silk carpets—the objectives of most visitors. The showroom is a converted air-raid shelter dating from the 1960s.

➕ K9 ✉ 44 Xingfu Dajie, Chongwen District 🕿 6715 1687 🕐 9:30–5:30 🚌 6, 35, 51, 60

TIANJIN

Serious antiques shoppers might consider a weekend excursion to Tianjin (▶ 20–1), where the antiques market takes over a part of Shenyang Dao in the center of town. Sunday morning from 8 to noon is the best time. Close to the first exit of the expressway from Beijing to Tianjin is the well-established Ming and Qing dynasty antique furniture store, C.L. Ma Furniture Co.

➕ Off the map, about 50 miles east of Beijing 🕿 022–2933 5555 🚌 Buses from Beijing railroad station

VAMBER ANTIQUE & ARTS HOUSE

This store, part private enterprise and part government-owned, declares that it specializes in "artificial antiques"— fakes at affordable prices, including some decent bronze and porcelain pieces. Packing and shipping can be arranged.

➕ G5 ✉ 29 Wusi Dajie, Dongcheng District 🕿 6401 0048 🕐 Mon–Sat 9–7:30 🚌 103, 112

XU CAI CHUN

Claiming to be the largest antique carpet dealer in Beijing, this store retails hand-made reproductions of antique carpets from Tibet, Mongolia and other exotic corners of China. Expect to pay around 500 yuan per sq. yard. Credit cards are accepted here.

➕ Off the map 🕿 Off Xiao Hong Men Rd. (south of the Third Ring Road) 🕿 6764 3063 🕐 9–6

Cloisonné

Cloisonné is an attractive, colorful enamel finish applied to many types of decorative ware such as lamps, vases, incense burners, tea sets, lanterns, tables, stools, prize cups and various silver-based items. It is produced by welding flattened wire on to a copper backing to form an outline. Enamel of different colors is then used to fill the outlined spaces with a range of rich shades. The Ming dynasty (1368–1644) was the heyday of cloisonné ware, but it remains popular today, and much modern work is based on traditional designs.

Arts & Crafts

Ceramics

The history of ceramics in China is as old as the civilization itself. The technology and art of design evolved from neolithic times, through the Bronze Age and all the great dynasties from the 6th century onwards. The Ming dynasty produced some of the most beautiful work through the use of under-glaze blue and white painting.

Old Peking

Two books first written in the 1930s by foreigners living in the city provide an insight into the old capital and its way of life. They are *Peking*, by Juliet Bredon and *In Search of Old Peking*, by Arlington & Lewisohn (both published by Oxford University Press). *Twilight in the Forbidden City*, written by Reginald Johnston, English tutor and tennis coach to the last emperor, Puyi, has also been republished by Oxford University Press.

ARTS & CRAFT STORE

This store in the prestigious World Trade Center retails fine china, carpets and an array of expensive *objets d'art*, and has its own foreign exchange counter.

🕀 N7 ✉ 1 Jianguomenwai Dajie, Chaoyang District ☎ 6505 2261 🕘 9:20AM–9:40PM 🚌 1, 4, 37

BEIJING JADE CARVING FACTORY

The wide selection of jadeware here ranges from magnificently ponderous examples of this renowned Chinese handicraft to the more luggage-friendly in size. Look carefully at some of the finer items, noticing how cleverly the differing shades of green are used in the design.

🕀 L9 ✉ 11 Guangming Lu, Chongwen District ☎ 6702 7371 🕘 9–5

CUI WEN GE ART SEALS STORE

Chops (► panel opposite), made from a variety of materials and to suit most budgets, are the specialty here. If you would like to have your name carved in Chinese, ask your hotel staff to write down the correct characters for you.

🕀 F8 ✉ Liulichangdong Jie 🕘 9–5 🚇 Hepingmen

EAST GALLERY

A small selection of mostly contemporary paintings, plus some old photographs at reasonable prices. There are a couple of similar stores close by.

🕀 M3 ✉ 28 Sanlitun Lu, Chaoyang District ☎ 6415 7314 🕘 10–7 🚌 115, 118

FORBIDDEN CITY SHOPS

Small shops inside the Forbidden City include a stall at the entrance to the Gate of Supreme Harmony that sells an inexpensive and attractive poster map of the palace complex. The most useful gift shop, simply called Gift Shop, just inside the north gate (where the rented audiotapes are returned), has a small but discriminating selection of art books, quality reproductions of Ming and Qing art, CDs, puzzles, theme umbrellas and other souvenirs. Next door, the bookstore with the grandiose title Books of Cultural Relics, Archeology & Arts has the city's best selection of translated academic titles on Chinese art and archeology. Other arts and crafts stores form a shopping corridor where you can find affordable gifts such as painted perfume bottles.

🕀 G5 ✉ Jingshanqian Jie, Dongcheng District 🕘 8:30–5 🚇 Qianmen

FRIENDSHIP JEWELRY STORE

Hardly anyone finds this place unless visiting the Ancient Observatory or arriving on a tour bus. The two floors are filled with display cabinets of gold and silver jewelry and precious stones.

🕀 K7 ✉ 2 Beijing Guguang Xiangtainei, Jianguomen Dajie ☎ 6527 4012 🕘 9:30–6 🚇 Jianguomen 🚌 1, 4, 52

FRIENDSHIP STORE

Before the government abolished the Foreign Exchange Certificate (FEC) system in 1995, foreign visitors had to use FEC for the purchase of anything important. The Friendship Store was then the major shopping venue for visitors; Chinese citizens were not even allowed inside. The store remains well worth a visit, if only to check the fixed prices and the range of items. There are four levels; all but the second floor, where there is a foreign-exchange facility at a branch of the Bank of China, offer a good range of arts and crafts: jade, porcelain, cloisonné, lacquerware, silk, linen, paintings, carpets, works of calligraphy, and kites.

➕ L7 ✉ 17 Jianguomenwai Dajie, Chaoyang District ☎ 6500 3311 🕐 9–8:30PM 🚌 1, 2, 3, 4, 9, 802

HONGQIAO MARKET

In the central area on the third floor, freshwater pearls hang by the hundreds from strings and are made up on the spot to customers' wishes. There are no fixed prices, so bargaining is required. Experts rub two pearls together; The rougher the contact the better; if they rub together smoothly the pearls are of poorer quality. Arts and crafts stores share the same floor. Some (Nos. 213–14 and 218) specialize in cloisonné (➤ 71); store No. 219 is devoted to finely crafted gilded-silver ornaments. Another area is devoted to antiques (➤ 70).

➕ J9 ✉ Tiantan Lu, Chongwen District 🕐 9–6 🚌 36, 39, 43

HONGSHENG MUSICAL INSTRUMENTS

The sign for this store is not in English, but it is easy to locate on the west side of Wangfujing. In addition to guitars and small brass instruments, there is a selection of traditional Chinese instruments—not easy to find outside China.

➕ H6 ✉ 225 Wangfujing Dajie, Dongcheng District ☎ 6513 5190 🕐 9–6:30 🚌 104, 103, 803

LUFTHANSA CENTER

The fifth floor of this large shopping plaza is devoted to arts and crafts and offers a wide choice of jade, pottery and porcelain and assorted collectibles. A separate room serves as a gallery for Chinese prints. Prices are fixed, but a 10 percent discount is still worth trying for.

➕ N2 ✉ 50 Liangmaqiao Lu, Chaoyang District ☎ 6465 1188 🕐 9–9 🚌 300, 402, 801

SCROLL ALLEY

Although way off the beaten track, this motley street market is easy to reach by subway. Walk east from Chegong-zhuang station, turning north when you see the stalls on your left. A good place to have pictures mounted as scrolls.

➕ D3/4 ✉ North of Ping'anlixi Dajie 🕐 9–5 🚇 Chegongzhuang

Chops

Name chops—personalized stamps— have been used for thousands of years in China and, despite mass literacy, are still commonly used. In a number of official situations, where the West would demand a signature, the Chinese will stamp a document with their personal name chop. The chops are made of a variety of materials—marble, jade, wood and even plastic—and the better arts and crafts stores will stock a range. It is easy to have your name put on one in Chinese characters or in your own language. When making a purchase, be sure to get an ink pad and ink—red has always been the traditional color.

CLOTHING

Bargaining

In Sanlitun and the Silk Market there are no fixed prices and bargaining is the rule. In general, try to bring down the vendor's first asking price before committing yourself to an offer and remember that you will always need to settle at a price above your first offer. A pair of Armani jeans should go for around 100 yuan, Caterpillar boots or a Gore-Tex jacket for around twice that.

ERMENEGILDO ZEGNA

This exclusive designer-clothing boutique is typical of the stores in the elegant Palace Hotel. Its neighbors include Versace and Boss. The prices are often higher than those in Europe, but wealthy Chinese customers have been known to turn up here with suitcases stuffed with cash and blow huge sums on a only a few garments.

⊞ J6 ☒ Jinyu Hutong, Dongcheng District ☎ 6512 8899 ◷ 10:30–9:30 ⊟ 110, 116, 120, 204

FRIENDSHIP STORE

You'll find clothing on the second floor. There is a terrific choice of silk by the yard, and the selection of traditional Chinese dress is worth a look. Come here and check the prices before trying your hand at bargaining in street markets.

⊞ L7 ☒ 17 Jianguomenwai Dajie, Chaoyang District ☎ 6500 3311 ◷ 9–8:30PM ⊟ 1, 2, 3, 4, 9, 802

GANJIAKOU

This market attracts few tourists because the clothes are entirely Asian in style, but it will appeal to those interested in investigating the latest fashions from Taiwan and Korea. Stalls line the street, Sanlihe Lu, as far as Baiwanzhuangxi Lu. Bargaining essential.

⊞ B4 ☒ Sanlihe Lu, Haidian District ◷ 9–5 ⊟ 102, 103, 114

HUFANG LU

Merchandise turns over quickly in this street market of busy clothing stalls, but European and North American visitors may well find most of the garments unfashionable. However prices are reasonable and occasionally worthwhile silk items turn up. Bargaining is essential.

⊞ F8 ☒ Hufang Lu, Xuanwu District ◷ 9–5 ⊟ 6, 14, 15

MILITARY SUPPLIES

This place, not far from the Jing Guang Center, stocks garments and gear of the People's Liberation Army (PLA), including heavy, double-breasted coats with gold buttons and PLA caps complete with red star.

⊞ N6 ☒ 23 Dongsanhuanbei Lu, Chaoyang District ◷ 9–5:30 ⊟ 9, 13, 117, 350, 402, 405, 801

RUIFUXIANG SILK AND CLOTH STORE

The areas around Dazhalan Jie (➤ 58)—a beehive of commercial activity for five centuries—is home to a number of interesting old stores, including the well-known Ruifuxiang, with its distinctive arched entrance and its façade decorated with storks. Raw silk, the main draw here, comes in a dazzling choice of colors, textures and patterns.

⊞ G8 ☒ 5 Dazhalan Jie, Xuanwu District ◷ 9–8 Ⓠ Qianmen

RUSSIAN MARKET

This is the unofficial name for the clothing market

that starts half-way up Ritan Lu and continues around the corner into Yabao Lu. Everything is geared towards the many Russian shoppers who arrive in Beijing on the Trans-Siberian railway with empty bags and return carrying or wearing as much as is humanly possible. Fur coats are a big draw—sable, mink, rabbit and fox—but there is also a fair selection of gloves, belts, scarves, women's garments and assorted other clothing items. The familiar designer names are not seen here, and the styles may seem garish to American shoppers, but there are bargains to be had. However, the vendors like to sell in bulk and may ask how many identical items you are interested in.

🚼 L6 ✉ Ritan Lu and Yabao Lu, Chaoyang District ⏱ 9–dusk 🚇 Jianguomen

SANLITUN LU

The Silk Market is by far the best known street for designer clothes, but a visit to Sanlitun Lu (▶ 59) may well prove equally gratifying. As the stalls are mainly on one side of a street, there is more space for walking, looking and trying on. The atmosphere is less hectic than the Silk Market and, often, better prices can be negotiated. The bulk of the merchandise consists of designer-label jeans, shirts, and women's wear. A couple of stalls sell shoes and, at the far end where wicker furniture is

sold, the stores continue around the corner to a fruit and vegetable market.

🚼 M3 ✉ Sanlitun Lu, Chaoyang District ⏱ 9–7 🚌 115, 118

SILK MARKET

A visit to this crowded market may convince you that very few visitors leave Beijing without having purchased a designer-label item of clothing or something in silk at a fraction of the store price. Silk Market is a small lane, off Xiushuidong Jie, crammed with stalls on both its sides. Shoppers, mostly visitors and expatriates, but some Beijingers too, fill every space and at times the atmosphere can seem frenzied. Apart from silk and cashmere, available at phenomenally low prices, bargains are to be had in Gore-Tex and down jackets as well as shirts, sweaters, raincoats, shoes and patchwork quilts. Famous brand names sit alongside impressive fakes and factory seconds. Be on your guard, and always check for imperfections.

🚼 M6/7 ✉ Xiushuidong Jie, Chaoyang District ⏱ 10–dusk 🚇 Jianguomen

YUANLONG SILK CORPORATION LTS

This is one of the oldest silk stores in Beijing, easy to find near the north entrance of Tiantan Park. A tailoring service is available

🚼 H9 ✉ Tiantan Lu, Chongwen District ☎ 6701 2854 ⏱ 9–5 🚌 34, 35, 36

Silk

Gorgeously embroidered silk shirts, blouses, lingerie, and bedspreadsmake ideal gifts. The Silk Market and the Friendship Store are both good hunting grounds, along with the large government-owned Beijing Silk Corporation, near the south gate of the Temple of Heaven. Bear in mind, though, that many items of silk clothing that seem such good value will never be the same after cleaning, even dry cleaning.

DEPARTMENT STORES & SHOPPING CENTERS

Shopping

Beijing's social revolution is nowhere more apparent than in the changed shopping scene. It is still possible to come across old state-owned stores whose surly staff give the clear impression that they don't want to be bothered by a troublesome customer with the audacity to wish to buy something. However, market forces are rapidly transforming everything, from store design inside and out, down to the new-minted smiles on the faces of helpful assistants. Most important, the shelves are now stocked with quality foreign-made goods and consumer items that were unknown a decade ago.

BEIJING DEPARTMENT STORE

It seems hard to believe that this store can survive for much longer in this prestigious location and in competition with Sun Dong An Plaza (► below). A little more than 10 years ago, this was Beijing's showpiece department store but now, upstaged by Beijing's newly arrived array of huge, smart shopping malls, its amateurish displays and general drabness puts it on a par with a cast-off statue of Lenin. See it while it lasts.
✚ H6 ✉ 255 Wangfujing Dajie, Dongcheng District ☎ 6512 6677 ⏰ 8:30–8:30 🚌 104, 103

CHINA WORLD TRADE SHOPPING CENTER

Chairman Mao would be appalled by this monument to yuppie consumerism. Among the chic boutiques and lifestyle stores is a well-stocked arts and craft store (► 72), a useful deli, a drugstore, and a large branch of the Hong Kong supermarket chain, Wellcome, which stocks an excellent range of local and Western foods.
✚ N7 ✉ 1 Jianguomenwai Dajie, Chaoyang District ☎ 6505 2288 ⏰ 9–9 🚌 1, 4, 37, 52

CVIK SHOPPING CENTER

Centrally located on Jianguomenwai Dajie and easily reached by subway, this stylish plaza is a Sino-Japanese joint venture whose stores sell a wide range of imported merchandise. Fast-food outlets in the basement.
✚ L7 ✉ 22 Jianguomenwai Dajie, Chaoyang District ☎ 6512 4488 ⏰ 9AM–9:30PM 🚇 Jianguomen

LUFTHANSA CENTER

This very large center houses one of Beijing's best supermarkets. A number of pleasant restaurants and cafés in the vicinity sustain weary shoppers.
✚ N2 ✉ 50 Liangmaqiao Lu, Chaoyang District ☎ 6465 1188 ⏰ 9–9 🚌 300, 402, 801

SUN DONG AN PLAZA

This is the big one, the glitzy flagship of the renowned and revamped Wangfujing. The 11-story plaza with three basement levels opened in 1998. Its 110,000 sq. feet of floor space includes department stores, clothing stores, an eight-screen cineplex, a food court, restaurants and an entertainment center.
✚ H5 ☎ 6527 6688 ✉ Wangfujing Dajie, Dongcheng District ⏰ 9–9 🚌 104, 103

VANTONE NEW WORLD SHOPPING CENTER

This glossy new mall is easily reached by subway and close to an interesting part of town (► 16). Many outlets are from international companies.
✚ D5 ✉ 2–8 Fuchengmenwai Dajie, Xicheng District ☎ 6858 8256 ⏰ Mon–Thu 9–9; Fri–Sat 10–10 🚇 Fuchengmen

CURIOS, CARPETS & COMPUTERS

BEIJING MARCO POLO CARPET

This elegant shop deals in new, handwoven wool carpets and silk rugs in a pleasing variety of designs. Prices range from 2,400 to 88,000 yuan (try for a discount). Shipping can be arranged.

✚ N7 ✉ L211, 2nd Floor, China World Tower, World Trade Centre, Jianguomenwai Dajie, Chaoyang District ☎ 6505 1974 ⏰ 9:30–9PM 🚌 1, 4, 37, 52

FOREIGN LANGUAGES BOOKSTORE

At one time this was Beijing's only store selling publications in English and other foreign languages. It still has the largest stock of such books in the city. As well as books and tapes in English and other languages, a range of dictionaries and other reference material is available in the Foreign Language Reference Bookstore at No. 219 Wangfujing (entrance through the Dunkin' Donuts shop).

✚ H6 ✉ 235 Wangfujing Dajie, Dongcheng District ☎ 6512 6922 ⏰ 9–8.30 (closes at 7PM in winter) 🚌 104, 211

SOUVENIR & BRIC-À-BRAC MARKET

A useful row of stalls near the Peace Hotel sells inexpensive Chinese gifts and mementos that make good souvenirs. Copies of the *Little Red Book* are originals from the Cultural Revolution, while the glitzy watches and musical lighters bearing the face of Mao are newly made.

✚ J6 ✉ Jinyu Hutong, Dongcheng District ⏰ 10–dusk 🚌 104, 106

STAMP MARKET

Asian stamps—some rare—as well as postcards and phone cards are on sale, and there are usually some stalls dealing in coins, including the old bronze ones with holes in the middle.

✚ Off the map ✉ Funite Furniture City, Beisihuanzhong Jie ⏰ 9–5 🚌 302

TIANTAN PARK MARKET

A covered corridor near the park's east entrance is filled with stalls displaying bric-à-brac and cultural curios from the 1960s. Look out for the ubiquitous Maoist clocks depicting revolutionary peasants holding aloft the *Little Red Book*.

✚ J9 ✉ East side of Tiantan Park, Chongwen District ⏰ 9–5:30 🚌 6, 15, 17, 20, 35, 39, 43, 106

ZHONGGUANCUN

Computer stores are concentrated here in the northwest of the city. (From Xizhimen subway station take a minibus along Baishiqiao Lu.) You will see the stores a couple of stops past the Friendship Hotel. A wide range of hardware, peripherals and software (beware— some is pirated) is available.

✚ Off the map, north of A1 ✉ Haidian Jie, Haidian District ⏰ 9–5 🚌 301, 303, 332, 333

Beijing books

The *Beijing Scene* guidebook (scene@well.com) is compiled by a group of expatriates (Beijing Scene Publishing, 400 Main St., Ansonia, CT 06401, USA) and is well worth dipping into for its wealth of informed and practical information. *The Forbidden City* by Mary Holdsworth and Caroline Courtauld (1995, Odyssey Press) is the most attractively produced book on its subject. *From Emperor to Citizen* (1987, Oxford University Press) is the autobiography of the last emperor, who lived in the Forbidden City until 1924. Good places to buy books on Beijing include the gift stores in the five-star hotels, notably the Swissotel (➤ 84), the Foreign Languages Bookstore (➤ this page) and two stores inside the north gate of the Forbidden City (➤ 72).

BARS & LICENSED CAFÉS

A fast-changing scene

Informal restaurants during the day and early evening, Beijing's licensed cafés gradually transform themselves into bars as the night goes on. Always call before heading off for the night—don't forget to ask your hotel to write down the name and address in Chinese for the benefit of taxi drivers.

ANNIE'S CAFÉ

Bring Your Own with a difference—you can bring your own food and prepare it for free in the kitchen. Few customers do, preferring to enjoy chatting over beers in this sociable sidewalk café/bar.

🔲 M4 ✉ Sanlitun Lu, Chaoyang District ☎ 6594 2894 🕐 11AM–2AM 🚌 115, 118

BLUE HAND

This little bar opposite the Kempinski Hotel is frequented by expatriates and foreign students who value the inexpensive beer and food. On warm summer nights, the outdoor seating is an added attraction.

🔲 N2 ✉ Liangmaqiao Lu, Chaoyang District 🕐 24 hours 🚌 300, 402, 801

CHAMPAGNE BAR

One of the better hotel bars in Beijing. The resident band, typically Filipino, jump-starts the evening around 7:30, after happy hour, and continues until 1AM. Reservations are available.

🔲 N5 ✉ Jing Guang Centre, Dongsanhuanbei Lu, Chaoyang District ☎ 6501 8888 ext. 2561 🕐 4PM–1AM 🚌 112, 113, 9, 402

COCO CLUB

Latin American music and food sets the scene in this comfortable hotel bar on Wangfujing. Early in the evening you can enjoy a game of darts or a quiet conversation, but when the band starts up, just sit back and enjoy the show.

🔲 H5 ☎ 6513 6666

✉ Prime Hotel, 2 Wangfujing Dajie, Dongcheng District 🕐 6–1:30AM 🚌 104, 111

FRANK'S PLACE

One of the first bars in the Sanlitun area, this remains a firm favorite with regulars. A good place to catch an international sports event on television.

🔲 M4 ✉ Gongrentiyuchangdong Lu, Chaoyang District ☎ 6502 2617 🕐 11:30AM–1:30AM 🚌 120, 117

GOOSE & DUCK

A passable imitation of an English pub, with Bass ale from the barrel. There is an extensive menu of Asian and Western dishes and live music most nights.

🔲 L6 ✉ 4 Ritanbei Lu, Chaoyang District ☎ 6509 3777 🕐 11AM–2AM 🚇 Jianguomen

HERE & NOW

This bar, very small but easy to locate opposite the Workers' Gymnasium, is worth seeking out for its arty *avant-garde* atmosphere. When the place is not crowded, you can appreciate the interior, which aspires to be a work of art.

🔲 L4 ✉ Gongrentiyuchangdong Lu, Chaoyang District ☎ 6416 0927 🕐 2PM–2AM 🚌 113

HOUSE BAR

Hard to know if this is a bar or just a licensed café. Either way it is worth a visit to sample the reasonable choice of drinks and the eclectic menu of American and

Asian dishes.

➕ M6 ✉ Guanghua Lu, Chaoyang District ☎ 6595 2485 🕐 11AM–2AM 🚌 28, 34, 48, 403

JACK AND JILL BAR

This friendly bar is typical of the new breed of bar opening in the Sanlitun area. The décor is bright and cheerful and the staff anxious to please. A pleasant place to relax in the evening after a shopping trip.

➕ M3 ✉ 52 Sanlitun Lu, Chaoyang District ☎ 6416 4697 🕐 6PM–late 🚌 115, 118

JAZZ YA

One of the best cocktail menus in this part of town draws local yuppies and expatriates from around the globe. The food is Western, while the jazz is international.

➕ M4 ✉ 18 Sanlitun Lu, Chaoyang District ☎ 6415 1227 🕐 11AM–2AM 🚌 115, 118

JOHN BULL

Brass fittings, dark wood and British Empire memorabilia—brass wallplates and Toby jugs—complement fish and chips and Yorkshire pudding in this mock-English pub. The first pub in Beijing to serve Guinness, John Bull, and Tetley's bitter on draft.

➕ L6 ✉ 44 Guanghua Lu, Chaoyang District ☎ 6532 5905 🕐 11AM–midnight 🚌 1, 4, 9, 802

MAGIC MUSHROOM

After a hectic twirl through the Silk Market

(▶ 75), this bar, conveniently located at the north end, offers a rest. At night a DJ often plays modern music to suit the style of the progressively modern interior.

➕ M6/7 ✉ Xiushudong Jie, Chaoyang District ☎ 6592 1446 🕐 6PM–2AM 🚇 Jianguomen

MINDER CAFÉ

All the basic ingredients for a good night out: decent bar food, live music, no cover, and a comfortable, spacious area to stretch your legs.

➕ M4 ✉ Nansanlitun, Chaoyang District ☎ 6500 6066 🕐 11:30AM–2:20AM 🚌 115

NASHVILLE

This country-and-western bar has live music most nights—"down-home" folks having a good time. Happy hour 5–8.

➕ M4 ✉ Dongdaqiaoxie Jie, Chaoyang District ☎ 6502 4201 🕐 2PM–2AM 🚌 115

OWL PUB

The main appeal of this upstairs bar is the large screen which shows a movie daily at 8PM, just when the happy hour comes to an end. The draft beer is especially reasonably priced. The entrance is next to the City Hotel.

➕ M4 ✉ 4 Gongrentiyuchangdong Lu, Chaoyang District ☎ 6592 6290 🕐 11AM–3AM 🚌 115, 113

PUBLIC SPACE

With its buoyant décor, air

Bar hopping

The Sanlitun Lu area is the only part of Beijing where you can bar-hop on foot. In addition to the the establishments mentioned on these pages, there are a host of other places in the vicinity. The small *hutongs* between Gongrentiyuchangdong Lu and Nansanlitun Lu (➕ M4) are alight with neon at night and more bars cluster behind the Swing bar at No. 58 further up Sanlitun Lu.

Beijing Internet

At the time of writing, the pioneering Keep in Touch bar (☎ 6462 5280), opposite the Kempinski Hotel (✚ N2), is the nearest Beijing gets to a cybercafé. Log in for a drink and an electronic chat (intouch@public3.bta.net.cn) open from 5PM to around 1AM. Live music and displays of Beijing student art add to the modernist mood.

of relaxed informality and tables on the sidewalk, this typical Sanlitun bar is buoyantly decorated and stays open until dawn if demand warrants.

✚ M3 ✉ 50 Sanlitun Lu, Chaoyang District ☎ 6416 0759 🕐 11AM–3AM 🚍 115, 18

REDWOOD BAR

The main attractions are the pool table, the dart board, and the live country-and-western music.

✚ N4 ✉ Gongrentiyuchangbei Lu (opposite Zhao Long Hotel), Chaoyang District ☎ 6462 9143 🕐 6PM–3AM 🚍 113, 117

RICHMOND BREWERY

The Richmond Brewery at 46 Dongdanbei Dajie (✚ J6) is easy to find, one block east of Wangfujing Dajie, but for atmosphere it is worth heading out to the northwest of the city to locate the second Richmond Brewery in Haidian, not far from Beijing University, usually packed with students.

✚ Off the map, north of A1 ✉ 29 Haidian Lu, Haidian District ☎ 6523 1039 🕐 10AM–2AM 🚍 301, 303, 332

SAN FRANCISCO BREWING COMPANY

The major draw is the selection of six microbrews (including raspberry ale). You can sample them before moving on to pints or take-home mini-kegs. A large screen shows

movies, accompanied by home-made sourdough bread and pizzas, and a decent selection of Cuban cigars.

✚ L4 ✉ West Wing, Beijing Asia Hotel, Xinzhong Jie, Chaoyang District ☎ 6500 7788 🕐 11:30AM–11:30PM 🚇 Dongsishitao

SCHILLER'S

This bar opposite the Kempinski Hotel has a reputation among the expatriate community and locals alike for friendly service and relaxed atmosphere. Food is served, and there are a few tables outdoors.

✚ N2 ✉ Liangmaqiao Lu, Chaoyang District ☎ 6461 9276 🕐 7AM–1AM 🚍 300, 402, 801

SHADOW CAFÉ

Out-of-center bar in the student area of Haidian, with surprisingly chic décor and jazz. On weekends there is usually some kind of live musical entertainment.

✚ Off the map, north of A1 ✉ 31 Kexueyuan Nanlu, Haidian District ☎ 6261 8587 🕐 8.30PM–2AM 🚍 301, 303, 332

WATER HOLE

The long happy hour (3–7PM) draws a regular crowd. With its good selection of quick meals, many merrymakers find little reason to move on during the course of an evening.

✚ M6 ✉ 3 Guanghua Lu, Chaoyang District ☎ 65074761 🕐 11AM–midnight 🚍 28, 43, 48, 403

CLUBS & DISCOS

CD CAFÉ JAZZ CLUB
The archetypal jazz club, smoky and dim, where you can relax and observe the city from an outdoor patio. Live musicians appear on weekends (small cover).

✚ N3 ✉ Dongsanhuanbei Lu, Chaoyang District (southwest of Museum of Agriculture)
☎ 6501 8877 🕐 9:30AM–2AM (closed on Mon & Tue) 🚍 300, 402, 801

FREEZER DISCO
The best hotel disco in the city, with live bands.

✚ Off the map ✉ Holiday Inn Lido, Jichang Lu, Jiangtai Lu, Chaoyang District ☎ 6437 6688 🕐 8PM–2AM (3:30AM at weekends) 🚍 401, 403

HARD ROCK CAFÉ
Rock memorabilia, pricey drinks and tasty barbecued pork chops and grilled fajitas. A resident band plays short sessions after 9PM, except Sunday, when there is a disco (cover).

✚ N2 ✉ 8 Dongsanhuanbei Lu, Chaoyang District (next to Great Wall Sheraton Hotel)
☎ 6590 6688 🕐 Sun–Thu 11:30–2, Fri–Sat 11:30–3, 🚍 300, 402, 801

NIGHTMAN DISCO
Only a few years ago, dance clubs were unknown in China, so although the Nightman may seem a little unsophisticated, it is still remarkable how exuberantly Beijingers have warmed to the genre.

✚ M1 ✉ 2 Xibahenan Lu (opposite west gate of International Exhibition Centre), Chaoyang District ☎ 6466

2562 🕐 8:30PM–2AM
🚍 302, 379, 18

POACHERS INN
Known for being rowdy—on weekends, after midnight, the place has more energy than the average bar due to the pulsing rhythms of its loud heavy metal rock music. Revellers often arrive here after decamping from more staid venues. Cover charge on weekends.

✚ N5 ✉ West gate of Tuanjiehu Park, Dongsanhuanbei Lu, Chaoyang District ☎ 6532 3063 🕐 10PM–5AM 🚍 115

SAN WEI BOOKSTORE
The floor above the bookselling area is a teahouse by day and a buzzing bar at night. The unusual décor suits the music, usually either live classical Chinese fare or laid-back jazz. Well worth a visit.

✚ E7 ✉ 60 Fuxingmennei Dajie, Xicheng District (opposite Minzu Hotel) ☎ 6601 3204 🕐 9:30AM–10:30PM
🚇 Fuxingmen

STORM BAR
This new bar in the north-east part of the city has a spacious dance floor, a discriminating bill of live bands, and balcony seating for those who prefer to watch. The local draft beer is reasonably priced.

✚ Just north of M1
✉ Zuojiazhuangbeilishangye Lu, Chaoyang District ☎ 6464 8988 🕐 7PM–3AM 🚍 302, 379

Food, drink and culture

On Sunday mornings at the Jianguo Hotel (✚ M7) on Jianguomenwai Dajie, a small classical orchestra provides a backdrop for a relaxing drink or meal. The atmosphere is pleasant, despite the setting in a hotel foyer, and if you feel like something a little louder, the adjoining Charlie's Bar is always lively and sociable.

ON STAGE

Acrobatics

The art of acrobatics—the physical feat and spectacle of gymnastic display—was practiced in China over 2,000 years ago and is still going strong. Training academies enroll students of primary school age, and it is not uncommon to see very young children performing alongside seasoned professionals. Each troupe develops its own program, blending vaudeville with gymnastics and acrobatics that require incredible training and concentration.

BEIJING CONCERT HALL

There is nowhere better to appreciate classical Chinese music than in the 1,000-seat Beijing Concert Hall, known for its excellent acoustics. Western music is also performed.

➕ F7 ✉ 1 Beixinhua Jie, Xincheng District ☎ 6605 5812 🕐 Evenings 🚇 Xidan

CHANG FU GONG DINNER SHOW

On weekends the New Otani Hotel hosts an evening's entertainment of Chinese music, acrobatic displays, a traditional Chinese play and a buffet dinner featuring both Western and Chinese food, including roast duck.

➕ L7 ✉ Hotel New Otani, Chang Fu Gong, 26 Jianguomenwai Dajie, Chaoyang District ☎ 6512 6106 🕐 7–9:30PM 🚇 Jianguomen

CHINA ACROBATIC TROUPE

This remarkable troupe, founded over forty years ago, offers one of Beijing's more enjoyable evening experiences. The repertoire encompasses plate stacking and spinning, tightrope walking, magic and juggling, interspersed with breathtaking gymnastic displays that are often packed with dramatic surprises involving bicycles or pieces of furniture. Highly recommended.

➕ N5 ✉ Chaoyang Theater, 36 Dongsanhuanbei Lu, Chaoyang District (opposite Jing Guang Hotel) ☎ 6507 2421 🕐 7:15PM 🚌 9, 113, 402, 405, 801

CHINA PUPPETRY THEATER

Chinese shadow puppetry is a dying art, so an opportunity to see a show at the China Puppetry Theater should not be missed, especially if a troupe from the countryside is performing.

➕ Off the map ✉ A1, Anhuaxili, Chaoyang District (off Beisanhuan Xilu, the Third Ring Road, in the north of the city) ☎ 6424 3698 🕐 Sat 10:30AM & 3PM; Sun 3PM 🚌 300, 302

EXPERIMENTAL THEATER FOR MODERN DRAMA

It is only since the death of Mao's fourth wife, an actress and the notorious leader of the Gang of Four, that the authorities have encouraged non-Chinese forms of theater. This hall is the main venue for such endeavors, and while some shows are in Chinese, international groups also perform in English.

➕ G/H3 ✉ Mao'er Hutong, Xicheng District ☎ 6403 1009 🕐 evenings 🚌 5, 107, 305

GLORIA SHOWCASE

A nightly show at the Gloria Plaza Hotel includes a roast duck dinner followed by magic, acrobatics, singing and traditional dancing.

➕ L7 ✉ Gloria Plaza Hotel, 2 Jianguomenwai Dajie, Chaoyang District ☎ 6515 8855 🕐 Dinner 6:30, Show 7:30 🚇 Jianguomen

HUAXIA CULTURAL AND MARTIAL ARTS CENTER

Different groups perform here on different nights of the week, perhaps staging a cultural narrative dance, like the traditional Chinese story of the Monkey King, or more often a display of martial arts. The Wushu, a fast and skillful performance of tai chi using swords, is a regular feature of the weekday evening shows.

🚇 H6 ✉ National Children's Arts Theater, Dong'anmen Dajie, Dongchen District ☎ 6512 9687 🚌 103, 104

LAO SHE TEAHOUSE

The Chinese cultural shows staged here nightly enliven excerpts from Chinese opera with comedy routines (in Chinese but highly visual), martial arts displays, acrobatics, unicycling and magic.

🚇 G7 ✉ 3rd Floor, Da Wan Cha Building, 3 Qianmenxi Dajie, Xuanwu District ☎ 6303 6830 🕐 7:40–9:20 🚇 Qianmen

LIYUAN THEATER

The Beijing Opera Troupe performs Chinese opera here daily. Screens alongside the stage carry English translations, and English program notes help you to appreciate what is going on during the show as you sit at the Ming-style tables sipping tea.

🚇 F9 ✉ Qianmen Hotel, 175 Yong'an Lu, Xuanwu District ☎ 6301 6688 ext. 8860 🕐 7:30–8:40 🚇 Qianmen

POLY PLAZA INTERNATIONAL THEATER

This is a major venue for ballet, music and opera—Puccini's *Turandot*, the New York City Ballet or the Beijing Jazz Festival.

🚇 L4 ✉ 14 Dongzhimennan Dajie, Chaoyang District ☎ 6500 1188 ext.5682 🚇 Dongsishitiao

ZHENGYICI THEATER

The history of this theater goes back to 1620, when it was first built as a temple. Converted into a hotel after 1949, then finally closed down, it was saved from demolition in 1994 by a millionaire opera aficionado who financed a lavish reconstruction. Today, there is nowhere better to watch Beijing opera. Admission usually includes tea and cookies (during the day, the theater is a teahouse).

🚇 F7 ✉ 220 Xiheyan Dajie, Xuanwu District District ☎ 6318 9454 🕐 Nightly performances 🚇 Xuanwumen

ZHONGHE THEATER

Though not such a magnificent theater as the Zhengyici (► above), the Zhonghe is also responding to the revival of interest in Beijing opera and is arguably the best place to experience this unique art form. It is now a regular venue for performances.

🚇 G8 ✉ 5 Liangshidian Jie, Chongwen District ☎ 6303 7083 🕐 Evenings 🚇 Qianmen

Chinese opera

This highly stylized ancient art form has only a passing resemblance to Western opera and leaves most Westerners utterly bemused. The richly costumed players mix dance and song with mime—accompanied by Chinese instruments. Some grasp of the basic plot will help in understanding the action. The usual five-hour performance is reduced to a mere 90 minutes for the benefit of foreigners, although full performances are rare nowadays. The shortest performances are at the Lao She Teahouse (► at left).

LUXURY HOTELS

Room prices

Approximate prices for a double room:

Luxury   over 1500 yuan
Mid-range   700–1500 yuan
Budget   under 700 yuan

Use your hotel

Beijing hotels offer one invaluable service apart from providing a room and shelter: they will write down your destination in Chinese for you to show to taxi drivers when you go out. Ask the doorman to make sure that the driver knows exactly where you want to go—and don't forget to take the hotel's own namecard with you for the return journey.

CHINA WORLD

Consistently one of Beijing's best hotels for its over 700 tastefully furnished rooms, superb restaurants and first-class gym, swimming pool and golf center with two golf simulators.

✚ N7 ✉ 1 Jianguomenwai Dajie, Chaoyang District ☎ 6505 2266; fax 6505 3167 🚍 1, 4, 37, 52

GREAT WALL SHERATON

In the Sanlitun diplomatic district, a short taxi ride from the city center, on the Third Ring Road. Built around a seven-story atrium loaded with creature comforts.

✚ N3 ✉ 10 Dongsanhuanbei Lu, Chaoyang District ☎ 6500 5566; fax 6500 1938 🚍 300, 402

HILTON

Over 300 rooms, convenient to the airport and the Sanlitun diplomatic and shopping district. Calm and attractive.

✚ N2 ✉ 1, Dongfang Lu, Chaoyang District ☎ 6466 2288; fax 6465 3052 🚍 300, 402, 801

NEW CENTURY

Good for families and sports-lovers. The recreation center includes a good-size pool, a bowling alley and outdoor tennis courts. Good transportation to the city center.

✚ A3 ✉ Shoudu Tiyuguannan Lu, Haidian District ☎ 6849 2001; fax 6849 1103 🚇 Xizhimen

PALACE

The Palace vies with the China World as Beijing's best hotel and exudes luxury in over 500 rooms, within walking distance of the Forbidden City. Chinese and Western restaurants, a pool, a health club and a dance club.

✚ J6 ✉ 8 Jinyu Hutong, Dongcheng District ☎ 6512 6192; fax 6512 7118; 🚍 103, 11, 106

RADISSON SAS

Terrific rooms, a good-size pool, tennis and squash courts and a Finnish sauna help make the Radisson popular, especially with Scandinavians. A large supermarket is next door.

✚ Just north of M1 ✉ 6A Beisanhuandong Lu, Chaoyang District ☎ 6466 3388; fax 6465 3186 🚍 302, 18

SWISSOTEL

Few hotels in Beijing have geared themselves so successfully and pleasantly to the needs of Western vacationers. A subway station is nearby, and the facilities are generally excellent, including those for visitors with disabilities. Airport shuttle bus, too.

✚ L4 ✉ Hong Kong Macau Center, Gongshi Tiao Lu, Choyang District ☎ 6501 2506; fax 6849 1103 🚇 Dongsishitao

MID-RANGE HOTELS

HOLIDAY INN DOWNTOWN
One of three Holiday Inns in Beijing, this one is conveniently close to a subway station and shopping malls. It has a good recreation center and an affordable Western-style restaurant.
✚ D4 ✉ 98 Beilishi Lu, Xicheng District ☎ 6833 8822; fax 6834 0696 🚇 Fuchengmen

MINZU
A good hotel in a useful location just west of the city center. Over 600 newly decorated rooms, plus a gym and a billiards room.
✚ E7 ✉ 51 Fuxingmennei Dajie, Xicheng District ☎ 6601 4466; fax 6601 4849 🚇 Xidan

OCEAN
Located in an up-and-coming Chinese commercial area whose nightclubs come alive with neon at night, this smart modern hotel is within walking distance of the Forbidden City.
✚ J6 ✉ 189 Dongsinan Jie, Dongcheng District ☎ 6522 8888; fax 6522 9564 🚌 110, 116

OLYMPIC
This gray monolith is stylish and contemporary and has rates that are almost in the budget category. The only drawback is the location, a bus ride and subway journey from the city center.
✚ A2 ✉ 52 Baishiqiao Lu, Haidian District ☎ 6217 6688; fax 6217 4104 🚇 Xizhimen

PEACE
This hotel at the top end of the price range, is in the heart of the city, with over 500 rooms, an indoor swimming pool, and both Western and Chinese restaurants.
✚ J6 ✉ 3 Jinyu Hutong, Dongcheng District ☎ 6512 8833; fax 6512 6863 🚌 104, 111

SONG HE
Well versed in the art of dealing with Western visitors and conveniently close to Wangfujing Dajie and the Forbidden City. Rooms are at the top end of the category.
✚ J5 ✉ 88 Dengshikou Dajie, Dongcheng District ☎ 6513 8822; fax 6513 9088 🚌 111, 108

QIANMEN
Not too far from the Forbidden City, the Qianmen has a chic lobby, good restaurants, a gym, sauna and billiard room. Rates are at the lower end of the price category.
✚ F9 ✉ 175 Yong'an Lu, Xuanwu District ☎ 6301 6688; fax 6301 3883 🚌 15, 25, 102

XINDADU
Also called the Beijing Mandarin, this upscale four-star hotel is in the north-west of the city, south of the zoo. It has a swimming pool, a sauna and fitness center, and several restaur-ants.
✚ B4 ✉ 21 Chegongzhuangxi Lu, Xicheng District ☎ 6831 9988; fax 6833 8507 🚇 Xizhimen

Rest assured
The days when hotel staff strolled into hotel rooms uninvited are long gone. The general standard of hotels that welcome foreign guests is high. When you choose accommodation in Beijing today, a hotel's location and availability of transportation to the city center are usually the most relevant considerations. (Apart from the Olympic and Xindadu, all the hotels on this spread are close to the city center.)

BUDGET ACCOMMODATIONS

Worth considering

Backpackers favor the Jinghua Hotel (☎ 6722 2211) on Nansanhuan Zhong Lu for its budget dormitory accommodation, inexpensive restaurants, economically priced tours to the Great Wall, bicycle rental facility and general willingness to provide information. The big drawback is its location, on the southern end of the Third Ring Road. Take bus 17 from Qianmen to the Haihutun bus station and walk from there.

DONG FANG

Very good value for a hotel with this level of facilities. Located in the Qianmen area, the Dong Fang has eight restaurants, a sauna and gym, a business center and a laundry. All 320 rooms are air-conditioned.

✚ F9 ✉ 11 Wanming Lu, Xuanwu District ☎ 6301 4466; fax 6304 4801 🚍 59, 105

FANGYUAN

Tucked away down a street off Wangfujing. Rooms are rather drab, but good value considering the central location.

✚ H5 ✉ 36 Dengshikouxi Jie, Dongcheng District ☎ 6525 6331 🚍 103, 104, 111

FAR EAST HOTEL

Affordable accommodation in the heart of the Dazhalan area, within walking distance of Tian'anmen Square. Chinese restaurant.

✚ F8 ✉ 90 Tieshuxie Jie, Xuanwu District ☎ 6302 8811; fax 6301 8233 🚇 Qianmen

FEIXIA

Backpackers like the budget doubles (under 200 yuan). Rooms with shared facilities cost less.

✚ C7 ✉ Building 5, Xiabanmenwai Dajie, Xuanwu District ☎ 6301 2228; fax 6302 1764 🚇 Nanlishi Lu

GUO AN

A 128-room hotel with air-conditioning, in an accessible location close to the city center and well served by buses. It also has a McDonald's.

✚ M5 ✉ 1 Guandongdianbei Jie, Chaoyang District ☎ 6500 7700; fax 6500 4568 🚍 109, 101, 110, 112

GUOTAI

The Guotai has a terrific location in the heart of the city and is favored by visiting Russians, who are within walking distance of their favorite market (► 74). Lots of facilities, including a cash-only currency exchange and restaurants near by.

✚ M7 ✉ 12 Yonganxili, Jianguomenwai Dajie, Chaoyang District ☎ 6501 3366; fax 6501 3926 🚇 Jianguomen

GUOZHAN

This modern hotel is an affordable option for anyone seeking budget accommodation within reach of good food—the Laxenoxen restaurant of the Radisson SAS Hotel (► 68) and a huge supermarket are across the street. The hotel has some 70 standard rooms with air-conditioning, and a Sichuan restaurant.

✚ Just north of M1 ✉ 10 Beisanhuandong Lu, Chaoyang District ☎ 6463 9922; fax 6467 9060; e-mail guozhan@public3.bta.net.cn 🚍 302, 379

RAINBOW

A decent modern Chinese hotel, with few foreign visitors and little English spoken, in the interesting Qianmen area. Restaurants include one offering medicinal cuisine and a Japanese restaurant.

✚ F9 ✉ 11 Xijing Lu, Xuanwu District ☎ 6301 2266; fax 6301 1366 🚍 59, 106, 343

BEIJING
travel facts

ARRIVING & DEPARTING

Before you go

- Visitors must hold a valid passport (with an expiration date at least six months after your planned arrival to China) and a visa.
- A single-entry visa is usually valid for 30 days and must generally be used within three months of issue. Visas are available through your country's Chinese embassy or consulate and through specialist tour operators.
- One-month visa extensions can be arranged through the Public Security Bureau ✉ 85 Beichizi Dajie ☎ 6525 5486.
- No vaccinations are required, but some doctors recommend inoculation against Hepatitis A.

When to go

- The best time to visit is between September and mid-November followed by April and May.

Climate

- There are four distinct seasons, with extreme temperatures in winter and summer.
- Freezing winds from Siberia can drop the temperature to 5°F from mid-November to March.
- April and May are dry, with a wind from the Gobi Desert blowing across the city.
- From June to August it is uncomfortably hot (around 80°F), and very humid.
- The weeks between September and mid-November have pleasant temperatures and little rain.

Arriving by air

- Capital Airport is 22 miles north of Beijing.
- The taxi fare into the city is around 100 yuan.
- Shuttle buses run every half-hour between the airport and the city. The fare is 16 yuan. There are two services, A and B, and between them they stop along the way near most of the big hotels. You can buy tickets on the bus and a route leaflet is available from the airport information desk.

Arriving by train/bus

- There are five railroad stations. The new West Railroad Station at Lianhuachi (✛ A8) handles routes to and from the south and west, including Hong Kong. There are no international bus routes, but four main stations serve buses to different parts of the country.

Customs regulations

- Authorization is required for the export of antiques (► 70). Chinese currency cannot be exported. Two liters of any alcohol may be imported.

Departure/airport tax

- 90 yuan departure tax.

ESSENTIAL FACTS

Electricity

- Current is 220 volts. Beijing sockets come in a bewildering variety of sizes and types and though big hotels can supply adaptors, it is best to bring your own.

Etiquette

- Confrontation or a public display of anger is counter-productive.
- Other public displays of strong emotion are not advisable.
- Avoid discussing Chinese domestic politics.

Insurance

- Check your policy and ensure you will be covered for medical emergencies, loss, theft, and the like

- In the event of illness or injury requiring treatment, try to obtain an English translation of any documents/receipts written in Chinese.

Money matters

- RMB (Renminbi) is the currency of China and the basic unit is the yuan, which is made up of 10 jiao (pronounced as mao), each of which is again divided into 10 fen. There are paper notes for 1, 2, 5, 10, 50 and 100 yuan, and the smaller 1, 2 and 5 mao. There are also coins for 1, 2 and 5 yuan, 1, 2 and 5 mao, and 1, 2 and 5 fen.
- Most major credit cards are accepted at hotels, and the number of smarter restaurants and stores where you can use them is increasing all the time.
- Travelers' checks are not only safer than cash, they also attract a better exchange rate. They can be cashed at branches of the Bank of China and at bureaux de change in hotels.
- As a rule, whenever prices are not displayed in writing, bargaining is probably expected. Politely ask for a discount. If the price still seems high, ask again. Bear in mind that once you make an offer, you will probably need to go above it eventually. Ask yourself whether the price difference you are bargaining over is really that much when converted to your own currency.

National holidays

- Jan 1 (New Year's Day)
- Chinese New Year/Spring Festival. This is governed by the lunar calendar and usually falls in late Jan or early Feb. Everything closes, so try to avoid this time.
- Mar 8 (International Working Women's Day)

- May 1 (International Labor Day)
- May 4 (Youth Day)
- Jun 1 (Children's Day)
- Jul 1 (Anniversary of Founding of Communist Party of China)
- Aug 1 (Anniversary of Founding of the PLA)
- Oct 1 (National Day)

Opening hours

- Banks and offices: Mon–Fri 9–5 (closed 1–2 hours for lunch).
- Shops: Generally 9–6, often later. Private stores stay open as demand warrants.

Places of worship

- Catholic: St. Mary's Church Nantang Cathedral (Southern Cathedral) ✉ Xuanwumendong Dajie, Xuanwu District ☎ 6602 5221.
- Protestant: Beitang/Northern Cathedral ✉ 33 Xishiku Dajie, Xicheng District ☎ 6617 5198.
- Church of Jesus Christ of Latter-Day Saints ✉ Capital Mansions, 4th Floor, 6 Xinyuannan Lu, Chaoyang District ☎ 6532 4251.
- Judaism: Weekly Sabbath services ✉ Capital Mansions, 3rd Floor, Capital Club Athletic Center, 6 Xinyuannan Lu, Chaoyang District ☎ 6512 6662/6505 3701.

Student travelers

- Generally, no discounts are available to student travelers.

Time difference

- New York is 13 hours behind Beijing; Chicago is 14 hours behind; Los Angeles is 15 hours behind. Beijing is 8 hours ahead of Greenwich Mean Time.

Tipping

- Tipping is not routinely expected, except for guides, who appreciate a small tip.

Toilets

- Hotels and better restaurants have Western-style toilets. Elsewhere expect Asian-style hole-in-the-ground toilets (dip and pour as well as flush). Outside better hotels and restaurants, standards of cleanliness are not those of the West.

Tourist offices

- There is no tourist information office but a tourist hotline ☎ 6513 0828 is available. Hotel staff are usually helpful with everyday questions like how to get somewhere by bus, where to find the nearest supermarket and so on. If they are not too busy, they may also check on opening hours and the like (▶ panel on page 6).

Visitors with disabilities

- Little or no provision is made for visitors with disabilities. However, Beijing's broad, smooth streets are more user-friendly than those of most other Asian cities.
- Public transportation is best avoided—the buses are overcrowded and jerky.

PUBLIC TRANSPORTATION

How to use the subway

- The subway runs between 5AM and 10:30 or 11PM on two lines. The main circle line runs beneath the Second Ring Road; the second line, of less use to visitors, runs west from Xidan. A short walk is necessary to connect from one line to the other.
- Station names are in English on the platforms and an announcement in English is made on the train as it approaches a station. The only problem you may have is trying to figure out in which direction a train is heading when it pulls into the station where you are waiting.

How to use the buses

- There is a bewildering variety of vehicles: red and white, blue and white, trolley-buses, double-decker buses and private minibuses that carry the same number as the bus route they follow. On minibuses, you can always get a seat, and the vehicle will stop anywhere along the route. Public buses are often horrendously crowded in contrast and only the few air-conditioned ones—like bus 801, which runs between the Lufthansa Center (✚ N2) and the junction with Jianguomenwai Dajie (✚ N7)— offer any comfort.
- Know your destination stop in Chinese—better still, have it written down.

Where to get maps

- The map that accompanies this book shows subway stations (in blue) and many bus routes (in red). Some hotel shops sell a Chinese/English city map that shows all the bus routes.

Types of ticket

- Subway tickets cost 2 yuan, regardless of the length of the journey, and are purchased inside the station.
- Bus tickets are calculated according to the length of the journey. The basic fare is 0.5 yuan and longer journeys cost 0.8 yuan. Tickets are purchased from the conductor, but often the buses are so crowded that you have difficulty even seeing him. Fares on minibuses range between 3 and 6 yuan depending on length of journey.

Taxis

- Taxis are plentiful and inexpensive and, along with the subway, provide the best means of getting around.
- There are different types of taxi. The least expensive are small yellow vans which are less comfortable than a bus. Stick with the regular small car taxis, whose meters start at 10.4 yuan for the first 3 miles and then increase at 1.6 yuan per half mile, or the plusher sedan taxis whose meters start at 12 yuan and increase at 2 yuan per half mile.
- Always ask someone at your hotel to write down your destination in Chinese and show this to the driver before setting off. Also ask your hotel doorman to make sure the taxi driver knows where you're going.

MEDIA & COMMUNICATIONS

Sending letters and packages

- The easiest way to send letters and postcards is to let your hotel do it for you.
- Sending packages is time-consuming and often frustrating since printed matter has to be wrapped by postal officials. Leave parcels open because they must be inspected at the post office.
- Smaller packages can be sent from most post offices. Larger parcels need to go from the main post office—the International Post Office (✚ L6 ✉ Jianguomenbei Dajie).

Telephones

- Local calls are free, and hotels usually charge only a nominal fee at most.
- The easiest and least expensive way to make an international call is to use a card telephone in a hotel. Cards come in denominations of 10, 20, 50 and 100 yuan and may be purchased from hotel shops and hotel business centers.
- Use business centers in hotels to send faxes. It does not matter if you are not a guest.

Newspapers and magazines

- The only Chinese newspaper in English is the *China Daily*. It carries domestic and international news and is readily available in hotels. On Fridays, the *China Daily* carries entertainment listings as well as details of special food promotions.
- Foreign newspapers like the *International Herald Tribune* and magazines like *Time* and *Newsweek* are available in hotel shops. French and German newspapers and magazines are available in some top-class hotels.
- *Beijing This Month*, an official tourist magazine, carries current listings. It is available through hotels.

Television

- Better hotels carry CNN, as well as Star TV from Hong Kong, which has some English-language programing.
- Check the *China Daily* for the times of the short English-language news broadcasts on state television channels.

EMERGENCIES

Emergency phone numbers

- Emergency numbers are answered only in Chinese:
- Police: 110
- Ambulance: 120
- Fire: 119

Embassies and consulates

- Australia ✉ 21 Dongzhimenwai Dajie
  ☎ 6532 2331
- Canada ✉ 19 Dongzhimenwai Dajie
  ☎ 6532 3536
- France ✉ 3 Dongsanjie, Sanlitun ☎ 6532
  1331
- Germany ✉ 5 Dongzhimenwai Dajie
  ☎ 6532 2161
- Ireland ✉ 3 Ritan Donglu ☎ 6532 2691
- Italy ✉ 2 Dong'erjie, Sanlitun ☎ 6532
  2131
- New Zealand ✉ 1 Dong'erjie, Ritan Lu
  ☎ 6532 2731
- UK ✉ 11 Guanghua Lu ☎ 6532 1961
- USA ✉ 3 Xishui Beijie, Jianguomenwai Dajie
  ☎ 6532 3831

Medical treatment

- Better hotels have their own med-
  ical services. Clinics with
  English-speaking staff that treat
  foreigners include:
- Hong Kong International Medical
  Clinic ✉ Swissotel (Hong Kong Macau
  Centre), Dongsi TiaoLu, Chaoyang District
  ☎ 6501 2288
- International Medical Clinic
  ✉ Lufthansa Centre, Regus Office Building,
  Room 106, 50 Liangmaqiao Lu, Chaoyang District
  ☎ 6465 1561
- Sino-Japanese Friendship
  Hospital ✉ Yinghua Donglu, Hepingli
  Beikou ☎ 6422 1122 ext.3411

Medicines

- Shops in top-class hotels have
  their own shops that often sell a
  range of simple medicines—most
  notably the Watsons store at the
  Holiday Inn Lido, Shoudujichang
  Lu (outside the city center,
  towards the airport). Some bigger
  supermarkets, like those in the
  Lufthansa Center and the China
  World Trade Shopping Center
  (▶ 76) are also worth trying. The
  International Medical Clinic (see
  above) has a pharmacy.

Sensible precautions

- Beijing is generally very safe.
- Pickpockets operate in crowded
  places like railroad stations and on
  buses. Keep small cash at hand,
  but always ensure your wallet or
  purse is secure.
- Leave money and important
  documents in your hotel room
  safe or safety-deposit box.
- Always keep travelers' checks
  separate from your record of their
  numbers, and note the emergency
  contact number in case of loss.
- Bring with you a photocopy of
  your passport and visa and keep it
  separate from the original.

LANGUAGE

- In general, the better the hotel
  the better the standard of English
  spoken and understood. On the
  street, you cannot rely on commu-
  nicating in any language other
  than Chinese. Although many
  people know a little English, it is
  useful (as well as courteous) to
  know some basic spoken Chinese.
- When setting out anywhere,
  always ask the hotel to write
  down the place and address in
  Chinese and carry your hotel card
  with its address in Chinese for
  your return journey.
- Chinese characters are rendered
  into the Latin alphabet by the
  official system of Romanization
  known as *pinyin*.
- The modern phonetic romanized
  form of Chinese is called 'pinyin'.
  It is largely pronounced as
  written, but note the following:
  a as in c*a*r
  c as in bi*ts* when an initial conso-
  nant
  e as in h*e*r
  i as in f*ee*t unless preceded by c,
  ch, r, s, sh, z, sh, when it becomes
  er as in her

j as in *gin*
o as in *ford*
q like the ch in *ch*in
s as in *s*imple
u as in oo in c*oo*l
w as in *w*ade, though pronounced by some as v
x like the sh in *sh*eep but with the s given greater emphasis
y as in *y*o*y*o
z as ds in li*ds*; zh as j in jam

Basics

yes	shi
no	bu shi
I don't understand	bu dong
Do you understand?	Dong ma?
when?	shenme shihou?
where?	nar?
telephone	dianhua
police	jingcha
toilet	ce suo
excuse me	dui bu qi
time	shijian
today	jin tian
tomorrow	ming tian
yesterday	zuo tian
morning	shang wu
evening	wan shang
afternoon	xia wu
left	zuo
right	you
south	nan
north	bei
east	dong
west	xi

Greetings, etc.

hello/how are you	ni hao
please	qing
thank you	xiexie
goodbye	zai jian
cheers!	gan bei
no problem	mei wen ti
I'm fine	wo hen hao
My surname is...	Wo xing...
I am from	Who shi...laide

Getting around

Where is...?	...zai nali?
taxi	chuzu che
airport	fei ji chang
train	huoche
bus	gong gong qi che
bicycle	xi xing che
ticket	piao
turn right	You zhuan
turn left	Zuo zhuan
I'm lost	Wo milule
hotel	fandina
room	fang jian
post office	youju
bank	yin hang

Medical

doctor	yi sheng
aspirin	zhitongpian
I'm sick	Wo sheng-bingle
hospital	yiyuan
pharmacy	yaodian

Shopping

how much?	Duo shao qian?
too expensive	tai gui le
a little cheaper	pian yi dian ba
gift	li wu
credit card	xin yong ka
postcards	ming xin pian
stamps	you piao
antique	guwu
silk	sichou
jade	yu
carpet	di tan
rice	mifan
beer	pijiu
coffee	ka fei

Numbers

0	ling	9	jiu
1	yi, yao	10	shi
2	er, liang	11	shiyi
3	san	12	shier
4	si	20	ershi
5	wu	21	ershiyi
6	liu	100	yibai
7	qi	200	erbai
8	ba	1,000	yiqian

INDEX

CityPack
Beijing

While every care has been taken to ensure the accuracy of the information in this guide, time brings change, and consequently the publisher cannot accept responsibility for errors that may occur. Prudent travelers will therefore want to call ahead to verify prices and other "perishable" information.

Copyright   © 1999 by The Automobile Association
Maps copyright   © 1999 by The Automobile Association
Fold-out map: © RV Reise- und Verkehrsverlag Munich · Stuttgart
                 © Cartography: GeoData

Published in the United States by Fodor's Travel Publications, Inc.
Published in the United Kingdom by AA Publishing

Fodor's is a registered trademark of Fodor's Travel Publications, Inc.

ISBN 0–679–00261–8
First Edition

FODOR'S CITYPACK BEIJING

AUTHOR *Sean Sheehan*
COVER DESIGN *Fabrizio La Rocca,*
           Allison Saltzman
VERIFIERS *Accuracy Language Services,*
           Beijing

CARTOGRAPHY *The Automobile Association*
           RV Reise- und Verkehrsverlag
COPY EDITOR *Julia Cady*
INDEXER *Marie Lorimer*
AMERICANIZER *Chester Krone*

Acknowledgments

Sean Sheehan would like to thank the following people in Beijing who helped with the research and writing of this guide: Rita Goh; Audrey Guo; Dennis Holmes; Veronica Ann Lee; Foued El Mabrouk; Greg Pringle; Zhang Qingyun; Li Tong; Phillipa Yule; Janet Zhang; Lin Zesheng.
The Automobile Association wishes to thank the following photographers, libraries and museum in the preperation of this book:
Ingrid Booz Morejohn/Picture Works 5a, 5b, 7, 8, 9, 11, 19, 20/1, 32b, 52, 53, 59; Robert Harding Picture Library 32a; Pictures Colour Library 28a, 28b; Neil Sketchfield 15; Spectrum Colour Library 18, 23a, 41a; Xu Beihang Museum 55
All remaining pictures were taken by Gordon Clements and are held in the Association's own Library (AA Photo Library) with the exception of the following pages: Ingrid Booz Morejohn 12, 20, 23b, 29b, 30a, 61a; Alex Kouprianoff 6/7, 17, 27, 29a, 30b, 34b, 47b, 61b, 87a.

Special sales

Color separation by Daylight Colour Art Pte Ltd, Singapore
Manufactured by Dai Nippon Printing Co. (Hong Kong) Ltd
10 9 8 7 6 5 4 3 2 1

Titles in the Citypack series

Beijing

The Citypack map covers the city in detail, while the Citypack guide gives you just the information you need to experience Beijing:

- The city's top attractions and the must-see sights at each

- Itineraries for walks and excursions

- The best museums and galleries, gates and halls, temples and churches

- The most explorable parks and neighbor-hoods

- Offbeat sights even locals don't know

- Restaurants, hotels, shopping, and nightlife—with pithy descriptions of each recommendation

- Best festivals and events

- Travel facts and tips on getting the most from your visit

The author: Sean Sheehan traveled extensively in China during his eight years as a resident of Southeast Asia. He is also the author of Fodor's CityPack Hong Kong.

VISIT US ON THE WEB AT WWW.FODORS.COM